MW00667857

DISCOVERING MUSIC

300 Years of Interaction in Western Music, Arts, History, and Culture

Carol B. Reynolds

with

Amanda Marsrow

Silver Age Music, Inc.
Bowie, Texas

© 2009 by Silver Age Music, Inc.

All rights reserved. No part of this book may be reproduced or transmitted in any form or by any means, electronic or mechanical, including photocopying, recording, or by any information storage and retrieval system, without permission in writing from the Publisher.

Silver Age Music, Inc.
219 N. Smythe St.
Bowie, Texas 76230

PRINTED IN THE UNITED STATES OF AMERICA

ISBN: 978-0-9819990-0-5

061511

Table of Contents

Unit Worksheets and Resources

PREFACE

I've been Discovering Music since childhood. It started with playing *Frankie and Johnny* on an old upright in the church basement with my guitar-playing father (who taught me that playing by ear was more fun than any toy). It expanded to learning Jimmie Rodgers songs from Daddy out by the picnic table, and ironing on Saturday afternoons with my mom to the accompaniment of the Texaco Metropolitan Opera Radio Broadcasts. It continued through years of practicing on the Baldwin Acrosonic placed in front of the picture window (so that I could at least watch the other kids playing outside!). It grew to the fulfillment of my strongest dream when, while researching my doctoral dissertation in Leningrad in 1981, I sat, stunned, beneath a blaze of 19th-century chandeliers and heard the legendary Evgenii Mravinsky conduct the Leningrad Philharmonic. And the discovery continues, bringing me directly to the creation of this course.

I've designed *Discovering Music: 300 Years of Interaction in Western Music, Arts, History, and Culture* to be rich in color and flexible in depth. Many people are lending their talents to this course, as you will shortly see. You will meet quite a few of them throughout the seventeen Unit Lectures. Wherever possible, you will see paintings, maps, graphics, or a visual representation of the topics in the lectures, and you will hear and see the making of music. The three CDs, produced by Naxos, bring a treasure-chest of performances designed to turn the historical facts into living sound. The Resource Book can be used as a gentle reminder, or a rigorous academic course in itself, to be uncovered layer by layer.

This course is a traditionally structured survey of three hundred years of Western Music and Arts, starting right before 1600 and ending at the edge of World War I. It is intended for those who want to begin, or extend, their knowledge of Western Cultural History by using music as a key. Many elements in the units have come directly from my classroom experience. At every step, I emphasize the critical need to understand music and the arts in their social and cultural context throughout history. And I share stories that, I hope, will open the way for you to Discover Music.

Behind the stories are the faces of countless dear students whom I've been privileged to teach—all of them part of my own education in life and learning. Many of them have grown to become extraordinary musicians, and some even appear in this course!

I am deeply indebted to music historian (and, I'm honored to say, former student!) Amanda Marsrow for her enormous contribution to this course. What a privilege it has been to work together during those very months as she and her husband were waiting on the blessing of their first child

To my many colleagues, how could I thank you all? Let me start with Professor Barbara Hill Moore, Michael Inman, Bob Falls, Dr. Michael Keyton, Major Jim Keene, Maestro Miguel Harth-Bedoya, Michael Shih, Timothy Reynish, Kim Campbell and the Dallas Wind Symphony, Meredith Browning, Richard Odom, Tara Emerson, Michael Conrady, Valeria Mignaco, Alfonso Marin, and Tom Abbott. Special thanks, too, go to Katharina Lengert, SFC Alvy Powell, Ernestine Sisneros, and Captain Scott O'Grady. Thank you Kirk Hunter, Harold Goad, Fr. David Allen (in spirit), Julie Harris, Ralph Harris, and Trustin Woolf, for the marvelous fiddle tunes.

Speaking of musical inspiration, I am indebted to you, Paul Cristo, for your sparkling music and your technical assistance. For the wisdom and good cheer of our designers CaraLea Willoughby and Karrie Ross I am most grateful. I thank you, Naxos of America, Randall Foster, and Nick Angiollini, for everything, including solving a problem that surely would have irritated Wagner.

And there's the category of special friends who have supported us all the way (and even fed us) starting with Joan Cantwell and Lois Harris, Dr. Paula Miller, Saundra Pass, Beverly Myers and Larry Cox of Nostalgia, and Geoffrey Moore. And a very special tip of the hat to you, Dr. Vance Cuthrell and Dr. Ava Stanzack, for provoking me into action!

Speaking of action, you are the man of action, Richard Sides. I hope you know how grateful we are to you. And for advice that kept the road straight, thank you Michael and Becky Baker.

But doesn't it always come down to family? I am grateful to my sister-in-law, Kathy Doherty, for jumping in at critical moments. And to you, my children Helen and Dennis, for great and varied assistance. That leaves me face to face with the strength behind this course, my producer, video editor, manager, visionary, and encourager: Hank, my husband, the most creative and dedicated man I have ever known. And surely the most patient.

May we all continue to Discover Music with joy!

CAROL REYNOLDS
BOWIE, TEXAS 2009

ABOUT THE AUTHORS

Carol B. Reynolds grew up in the mountains of Virginia. A pianist, she became fascinated with Russian culture as a teenager. After completing a Bachelor's (Hollins College) and a Master's Degree (University of North Carolina) in Piano Performance, she embarked upon a doctorate in musicology. She lived in both the Soviet Union and Germany while completing her dissertation (Ph.D. The University of North Carolina, 1984) and taught in North Carolina and in Oregon. She joined the faculty of Southern Methodist University in 1985, where she became a Professor of Music History, teaching and publishing in the areas of opera, keyboard repertory, and Russian culture. She worked intensively with the International Students' Program, and in 2001 founded Southern Methodist University's study abroad program "SMU-in-Germany." She took a *very* early retirement after she and her husband Hank chanced upon a wonderful ranch in Montague County, Texas. They decided to embark upon two new adventures: "hobby ranching" (goats and cattle) and the development of new fine arts curricula. She continues to write, speak, and create educational materials for a variety of arts organizations. Her husband is a copyright attorney who holds a Ph.D. in Music Theory and two Masters degrees in Music. They have two grown children.

Amanda Lea Marsrow is the eldest of nine homeschooled children. Born in Lincoln, Nebraska in 1980, she grew up on a farm, and practiced her sheep-ranching skills side-by-side with her piano and her academics. She earned a Bachelor's degree in Music History and Literature in 2003 from Baylor University, a Master's Degree in Piano Performance from Southern Methodist University in 2007, and a second Masters Degree in Music History, also from Southern Methodist University, in 2009. Her Master's Thesis "Searching for Symbols: Symbolism in 'Silver Age' Russia, 1861-1917" combined her research interests in Music History, Piano Literature, and Russian History. Her husband Casey is a clarinetist and a member of the U.S. Army Band, stationed in Ft. Jackson, South Carolina. While working on the Resource Book for *Discovering Music,* Amanda and her husband were awaiting the birth of their first child, Asher.

FOREWORD

I commend you for including *Discovering Music* in your learning plan this year! An inspiring and informative journey awaits you, for I consider Dr. Reynolds to be one of the most effective teachers I have ever known. How I wish that such a resource had been available during the years my wife and I were homeschooling our five children, or, for that matter, in the many times I have taught introductory music history courses on the college level!

During the eight years Dr. Reynolds and I served as colleagues at Southern Methodist University, our office doors stood a few feet down the hall from the main music history classroom. I cherish fondly the memory of her classes letting out: of chattering students pouring past my open office door, some bounding with enthusiasm and others staggering with minds "blown" by the breadth and depth of what they had just learned. A short time later Dr. Reynolds herself would pass by, handouts and student essays a-flutter in the crook of one arm while with the other she towed a red Radio Flyer wagon overflowing with scores, recordings, books, and primary source materials.

Why does Dr. Reynolds inspire such learning and enthusiasm among her students? It is clear that at the heart of her effectiveness lies a deep passion for sharing knowledge about music. But passion, while necessary, is not sufficient for excellent teaching. A clue is provided by that red Radio Flyer wagon. Dr. Reynolds has never been one to "teach the textbook." Rather, she encourages students to learn directly from an abundance of primary and secondary sources, from live performances, from expert guests, and even, when possible, from "field trips" to Europe, where she herself has spent much time living. Her rich approach stimulates critical thinking and enables students to make their own direct connection with the past—an awareness of "the presentness of the past." This integrative approach means that her students don't simply learn about music, they also learn how music relates to other aspects of history and culture. When students think integratively, they discover that knowledge comprises not a static list of facts to master, but rather a dynamic and ongoing process of growth and discovery. And that is something to be excited about!

This very notion—that music *is* related to every other aspect of history and culture—is one that modern education has all too often forgotten. When school budgets are cut, music and the other arts are often first to go, because they are perceived as peripheral rather than central to learning. Earlier eras, however, regarded the study of music as integral to personal formation. The ancient Greeks, for example, included music among the seven liberal arts—so called because they represented areas of learning that every free citizen should possess. When the Greek liberal arts tradition passed into the Latin West through the writings of Martianus Capella, Boethius, and other writers around the 5th century A.D., it exerted a profound and lasting influence on Western Christian thought. In the writings of Boethius, for example, "music" encompassed much more than what we think of music today. Boethius divided music into three types. The highest of these is *musica mundana*, the "music of the spheres," the mathematical harmony that governs heavenly bodies, the seasons, and the cosmos as a whole. Second is *musica humana*, the harmony that governs the human body and soul. Third is *musica instrumentalis*, music made by voices or instruments, which renders audible the same principles of order evident in the cosmos and human beings. Although our understanding of the cosmos and of the human body has come far since the fifth century A.D., music remains a powerful construct for understanding our world.

Music also offers us a key to understanding ourselves. Music's power derives in part from the ways it expresses every aspect of what it means to be a human being. As human beings made in the image of God, we are spiritual, creative, relational, volitional, rational, emotional, and physical. Music integrates these facets of our humanity, not only making us more whole as persons, but also connecting us to one another in community. Through music the trinity of composer, performer, and audience can share intense communion of movement, thought, and feeling. Music both expresses and shapes virtually every aspect of our human identities, including our culture, ethnicity, race, nationality, gender, generation, and religious affiliation.

Because music itself is so deeply integrative, the study of music needs also to be approached integratively. This is precisely what Dr. Reynolds's course offers, in a way that has never been done before. Through the medium of video, this veteran of the college classroom integrates discussion of musical works, composers, primary sources, guest experts, and visits to historical sites. I warmly commend to you Dr. Reynolds's *Discovering Music* course. Happy learning!

DR. MICHAEL DODDS
HEAD OF MUSIC HISTORY
UNIVERSITY OF NORTH CAROLINA SCHOOL OF THE ARTS

HOW TO USE THIS RESOURCE BOOK

This resource book is designed to provide an outline for unit studies that will serve as a supplement to the *Discovering Music* **DVD Lectures** and **CD Listening Set**.

Each unit is constructed to present the music of a particular cultural era, phenomenon, or composer. Rather than attempt a comprehensive history of Western Art Music (what is often loosely labeled "Classical"), this course seeks to introduce and analyze significant musical developments within the social, historical, and cultural contexts that fostered them. The premise is simply this: music, or any creative product, does not occur in a vacuum. It is more often the outpouring of education, training, priority, and values of human beings. Even the most *intimidating* music has often come about for the most practical—even *humble*—of reasons! Understanding these reasons can change completely how we perceive this art.

Discovering Music seeks to present music in its "original habitat," historically speaking. Our hope is that gaining an understanding of this "habitat," along with a greater awareness of music's interaction with the fields of literature, visual art, history, and technology, will equip students for a wealth of musical experiences. And this understanding will be a powerful tool to unlock academics, culture, and history.

The **Figures, Places, and Dates** chosen for each unit are intended to provide students with "hooks"—concrete pieces of information that will offer a foundation of historical knowledge or additional historical perspective, depending upon a student's age or grade level. The **Vocabulary** sections are intended to supplement and support terms or concepts presented in the DVD Lectures. The **Listening Suggestions** presented in each unit are provided as guides for further listening for the most significant composers or genres presented within each unit.

FIGURES

The initial building-block of each unit is a list of the historical figures that appear most prominently in the context of the unit. The lists include composers, relevant political figures, scientists, philosophers, authors, artists, and performers. Nearly every name will be mentioned specifically within the DVD Lectures. Those few listed but not mentioned in the DVDs are useful to the unit's topic and can be researched separately. You may wish to:

- incorporate some (or all!) of these figures into a timeline
- select certain individuals whose dates you wish to memorize

- research individuals relevant to your studies in other subject areas

- search for resources (books, movies, documentaries, etc.) on these individuals at your local library

PLACES

Each unit contains a list of relevant geographical locations. Students should be able to locate these places on a map. They may also wish to research the history of a particular city or even a broader geographical region. Although the scope of this course necessitates certain limits, students will notice that many places—for instance, Paris, France, or Vienna, Austria—appear repeatedly and could easily fill a unit by themselves!

VOCABULARY

These definitions are intended to reinforce and clarify the information presented in the DVD Lectures. They are not intended to replace the student's consultation of a good dictionary or encyclopedia. Because so many music and cultural terms are in foreign languages, take advantage of the translations and explanations provided; many times, when encountering a term in a foreign language, it is helpful just to be able to "see" the word in print and associate the pronunciations in the lecture with the way a word looks on the page.

Be sure to know all vocabulary words and their definitions prior to taking the Unit Quizzes.

DATES

One of the most effective ways to learn and retain history is through developing associations. The chronologies presented in each unit attempt to place the topics within a particular historical setting. Dates concerned with musical events are placed in **bold-face type.** Special effort has been given to ensure that American history receives attention as well. Please note: these sections are NOT designed to outline any one composer's biography or to give a complete picture of any era of history. We urge you to make your own timelines and circles of key dates wherever possible. You may also wish to:

- select certain major events from this section to memorize
- incorporate some (or all!) of these events into a grand timeline that covers the entire period of the course
- perform additional research on specific wars, battles, or conflicts

- check for additional information on the time span presented in each unit on one or more of the historical timeline web resources listed in the "General Web Resources" page

LISTENING

Choosing selections for the accompanying CD Listening Set proved to be one of the most challenging aspects of *Discovering Music*. We are only too aware of the endless possibilities that could have been included! Happily, it has become comparatively easy, in our modern day, to access music via on-line services, many of which can be subscribed to at a reasonable cost. You may wish to explore these, starting with the Naxos Music Library (the world-wide company that produced the CD Listening Set for this course) at www.naxos.com.

For this course, however, begin with the pieces on your CD Listening Set. These appear in **bold print** in the **Listening** lists contained in your book. Be sure to spend sufficient time listening to those pieces (multiple listenings). Try to understand how and why they are presented within each unit in the DVD Lectures. See if you can hear some of the qualities discussed in the unit lectures.

After that, prepare to explore! Do not feel pressured, however, to locate and listen to every piece in the suggested listening. It is *far* better to know a few pieces well, than to trudge dutifully through a list of pieces, without gaining much understanding of them.

You may also wish to:
- listen to all of the remaining movements of a multi-movement work
- choose the works (from online lists of composers' works) that most interest you
- concentrate on a particular *genre* that appeals to you (concerto, symphony, arias, choruses, etc.)
- determine which types of instrumental or vocal sound appeal to you
- find music of other composers who were writing during the same time

WEBSITES

With the help of your online search-engine, you can search the world for information on every person, place, or idea presented in this course. We have sought to present you with only the most accurate, well-maintained, and useful sites. The online resources listed within each unit provide a wealth of information; they are annotated to help guide you to those you will find most helpful.

Although the best way to achieve maximum results from *Discovering Music* would be to visit each site, you can control the time and intensity

required to complete the course by limiting your viewing to one site per annotation. Every precaution has been taken in researching the sites listed. Depending upon your Internet security settings, students should be able to visit the vast majority of sites without encountering questionable advertisements.

Parents, please note: A great deal of art history revolves around depictions of the human body. Please be aware that many of the art websites show figures in various states of undress. As the course progresses closer into and through the 19th century, students are more likely to encounter adult themes and images. Some websites related to 19th-century poets also carry a note of warning. Although the "questionable" topics presented are not much different than what one encounters daily on TV or in the news, we want parents to be aware of what their students may encounter.

Please note, also, that websites annotated as a resource "Older students may wish to view . . ." are simply more *academically* sophisticated. These sites are "safe" but perhaps too *deep* for younger students and are intended mostly for those who may have developed a special interest in the related topic.

PUTTING IT ALL TOGETHER

The questions and projects listed in this section are a guide to synthesizing the information presented in each unit. Depending on the student's grade level, and level of interest, you may wish to choose one activity per unit or you may attempt them all. **Read through the questions and projects in this section before beginning your online research.** Several of the questions are directly related to the websites you will visit, and will help point students towards the most relevant information. **Questions in this section that are related to specific individuals will require visits to all of the websites attached to that individual's annotation.**

VIEWING GUIDES

To get the most out of *Discovering Music*, we recommend watching each lecture a minimum of two times. Viewing Guides are drawn entirely from the lectures, and are designed to give students a way to take notes and keep track of the most relevant information while viewing the DVD lectures. They may also serve as a more advanced unit quiz for some students. Suggested answers are given, including multiple answers where needed.

UNIT QUIZZES

The **Unit Quiz** for each chapter is found in the back of the book. The quiz draws from all sections of the workbook, as well as from the DVD. Answers are given, including multiple answers where needed. But keep in mind that, in many cases, additional answers can be correct. Describing music and the arts is not an exact science. Students may wish to design their own unit quizzes. It's excellent academic practice to do so!

Video Timings

Disc 1

Unit 1	Using Music History to Unlock Western Culture	44:56
Unit 2	Music Entwined with Great Events in Western History	41:56
Unit 3	Technology, Terminology, and Cultural Perspective	25.35

Disc 2

Unit 4	Fanfare and Power: the Court of Louis XIV	34:01
Unit 5	Sweeping Away the Renaissance into the Baroque	48.18
Unit 6	Liturgical Calendar, Street Parties, and the New Church Music	27:31

Disc 3

Unit 7	A Lively Journey through the Life of Johann Sebastian Bach	50:56
Unit 8	Enlightenment, Classicism, and the Astonishing Mozart	58:26

Disc 4

Unit 9	Into the Abyss: the Century Struggles with Unfettered Imagination	58:06
Unit 10	Beethoven as Hero and Revolutionary	37:48

Disc 5

Unit 11	Salons, Poetry, and the Power of Song	49:07
Unit 12	A Tale of Four Virtuosi and the Birth of the Tone Poem	53:09

Disc 6

Unit 13	Nationalism and the Explosion of Romantic Opera	56:05
Unit 14	The Absolutely New World of Wagner	35:48

Disc 7

Unit 15	Imperial Russia – A Cultural Odyssey	58:35
Unit 16	Load Up the Wagons: the Story of American Music	1:01:36

Disc 8

Unit 17	Turning the Page on Western Tradition with the Explosion of War	1:00:43

Total time: 13:22:36

DISCOVERING MUSIC

*300 Years of Interaction in
Western Music, Arts,
History, and Culture*

DISCOVERING MUSIC
Circle of Key Dates

LEGEND

♪ - Music Date
✦ - Military or Other World–Event Date

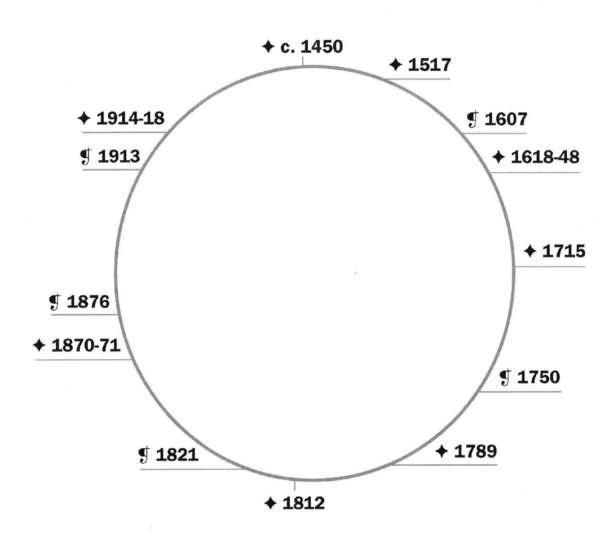

✦ c. 1450

✦ 1517

✦ 1914-18

♪ 1607

♪ 1913

✦ 1618-48

✦ 1715

♪ 1876

✦ 1870-71

♪ 1750

♪ 1821

✦ 1789

✦ 1812

Key to the Circle of Dates

1450
: A good ballpark figure for the beginning of the printing press. Gutenberg, working in Mainz, Germany, had been developing his press for years, but he made significant advances in typography in 1450. These laid the groundwork for printing his famous Gutenberg Bibles.

1517
: On October 31, Martin Luther nailed the *95 Theses*, or 95 statements of theological protest, to the door of the Wittenberg Cathedral, intending to address abuses, but ultimately setting the split of the Western Christian Church into motion (Protestant Reformation).

1607
: Claudio Monteverdi's opera *Orfeo*. The earliest opera still regularly produced. It is considered a landmark in the development of Baroque style, although it is heavily rooted in Renaissance musical and theatrical traditions.

1618-1648
: The Thirty Years' War. The bloody struggle to determine whether Europe would be Protestant or Catholic. In the end, the Southern regions remained primarily Catholic, and Northern areas turned primarily Protestant. Since the war lasted 30 years, these are easy dates to learn!

1715
: The death of the Sun King, Louis XIV. His descendents continued to build the palace of Versailles, and to nourish French arts, but nothing matched the personal and dynastic glitter of Louis XIV'x court.

: n.b. Just in case you find yourself confusing 1517 and 1715, remember that Martin Luther was a long-ago Renaissance figure, while Louis XIV was practically a modern man.

1750
: Death of Johann Sebastian Bach.

1789
: The French Revolution. All European monarchs are "put on notice."

1812
: Napoleon's defeat in Russia (many of his famished troops froze during their retreat back to France). The Battle of Waterloo three years later (1815) is considered the final victory over Napoleon.

1821
: Premiere of Carl Marie von Weber's *Der Freischütz*, or *The Free Shot*. It was not the first German-language spoken-dialogue opera or even the first opera based on magic (after all, Mozart's *The Magic Flute* in 1791 qualifies on both accounts). But it offered authentic German folk music and wove German folklore and legend together. It also

featured the trendy "spooky" elements, including the "Wolf's Glen Scene" that, even today, can send a shiver down one's spine.

1870-1871   The Franco-Prussian War, the first great *modern* clash between the French and the Germans.   The Germans won, and thoroughly humiliated the French with insufferable peace terms. The treaty was signed in the Hall of Mirrors at Versailles, which was a further slap in France's face. The momentum from this victory led the Germans finally to unite their many regions, kingdoms, and free trade cities into a real nation, with a central government, and a constitution. From this point on, it's possible to refer to the German nation or country of Germany, i.e. Deutschland. Otto von Bismark, known as The Iron Chancellor, was the master diplomat whose name emerged from this period, and his clever strategies kept Europe at peace for decades.

1876   The first performance of all four of Wagner's operas for *The Ring*— his famous tetralogy of operas.   This performance in August inaugurated his completely original and innovative new theater at Bayreuth.   It was attended by many famous people, including Tchaikovsky. Even today, the summer festival of Wagner's operas at Bayreuth is a major event.

1913   The premiere of one of the most radical pieces of music ever written, a ballet on a primitive Russian theme by Igor Stravinsky called *Rite of Spring.* Its premiere in Paris was famously marked by audience protests. The innovative young choreographer who designed this ballet, Vaslav Nijinsky, is sill famous to this day for the complex, strange new movements he taught his dancers.

1914-1918   The official dates of World War I, pitting Germany and her allies against France and her allies, ultimately including the United States. Germany was defeated, stripped of territory, and of what few resources remained after the devastating war. The peace treaty was signed in June 1919, again in the Palace of Versailles—an inversion of the situation at the end of the Franco-Prussian War.

Your Circle of Key Dates

Create your own LEGEND symbols

- **Music Date**
- **Military or Other World Event Date**
- **Other Significant Events**

DISCOVERING MUSIC TIMELINE

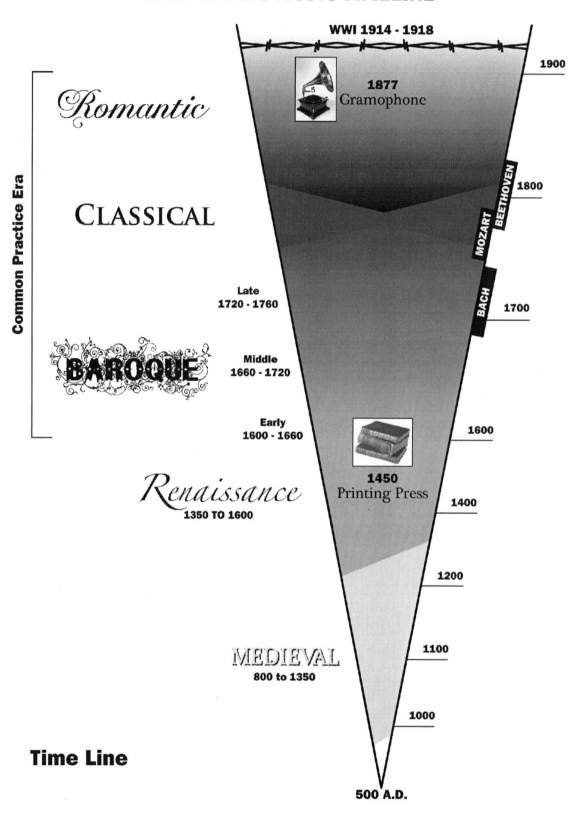

WWI 1914 - 1918

1900

Romantic

1877
Gramophone

BEETHOVEN

1800

MOZART

CLASSICAL

BACH

1700

Late
1720 - 1760

Common Practice Era

BAROQUE

Middle
1660 - 1720

Early
1600 - 1660

1600

1450
Printing Press

1400

Renaissance

1350 TO 1600

1200

MEDIEVAL
800 to 1350

1100

1000

Time Line

500 A.D.

YOUR TIMELINE

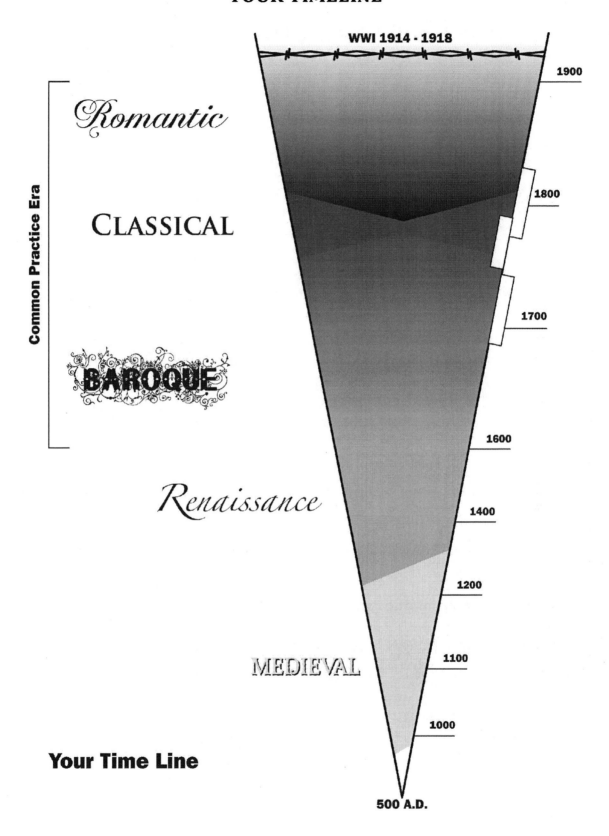

WWI 1914 - 1918

1900

Romantic

Common Practice Era

Classical

1800

1700

BAROQUE

1600

Renaissance

1400

1200

MEDIEVAL

1100

1000

Your Time Line

500 A.D.

THREE MEGA-COMPOSERS

JOHANN SEBASTIAN BACH   1685-1750

THEMES: LATE BAROQUE STYLE
CHURCH MUSIC
CANTATAS, CHORALES AND ORATORIOS
ORGANS AND TECHNOLOGY
LIFE AS KAPELLMEISTER

WOLFGANG AMADEUS MOZART   1756-1791

THEMES: CLASSICAL STYLE
ENLIGHTENMENT IDEALS
ITALIAN TRAINING
FORTEPIANO
OPERA

LUDWIG VAN BEETHOVEN   1770-1825

THEMES: ROMANTICISM AND REVOLUTION
STRUGGLE FOR INDIVIDUAL EXPRESSION
RISE OF NAPOLEON
HEILIGENSTADT TESTAMENT
GOETHE

UNIT 1

USING MUSIC HISTORY TO UNLOCK WESTERN CULTURE

FIGURES

The Beatles
George Harrison (1943-2001), John Lennon (1940-1980), Paul McCartney (b. 1942),
Ringo Star (b. 1940)

Plato
(c. 427-c. 347 b.c.)

Charles Dickens
(1812-1870)

Thomas Edison
(1842-1931)

Robert Schumann
 (1810-1856)

Clara Wieck Schumann
(1819-1896)

PLACES

Queens Peak, Montague County, Texas

VOCABULARY

Ears, Brains, Imagination
A phrase you'll hear several times in the course of this study. Each is needed to understand and make use of music (and cultural) history.

45 rpm
A flat recording disc that rotated (spun) 45 times per minute. It held approximately 3 minutes of sound.

I-pod
A device for playing "media" (songs, movies) developed and marketed by Apple Inc. and launched in 2001.

Score
The written-down version of musical notes.

Song
A piece of music with words meant to be sung. Songs ordinarily begin with the words (text) and, hence, a phrase often quoted in music: *prima le parole, e dopo la musica* (first the words, then the music). There are occasional examples in the 19th and 20th centuries of instrumental pieces with no words that are called "Songs without Words."

Opus
Latin for work, as in creative work.

Opera
The Italian singular for *opus* (work, creative work). The plural is *opere*. By extension (after 1600) *opera* came to mean a staged, sung dramatic work.

Movement
A distinct section of a piece of music.

Attacca (*attaccare* = to begin or start into)
Italian instruction placed at the end of a movement. In music, *attacca* means "to attack" or jump right into the *next* movement with no pause.

Tempo
The speed of a piece of music. From the Latin for time (*tempus*)

Gramophone
The first working model was invented by Thomas Edison in 1877. Many inventors world-wide were interested in the idea. Edison's gramophone recorded sounds on tubular **waxed cylinders**. Another important inventor, Emile Berliner, perfected

recording on flat discs similar to records. Ultimately, Berliner's idea won out. Gramophones were acoustical, meaning all sound went into a horn and was recorded via a needle onto a surface. The playback reversed the process. The gramophone was powered, ultimately, by cranking a wind-up mechanism. There was, of course, no electricity and no electronic amplification.

Acoustics
The science of sound and hearing.

Register
Within any instrument or voice, the full scope (from high to low parts) of the notes that can be sounded. A piano has a large register (88 notes), while a human voice has a much smaller, or narrower, register.

LISTENING

The Beatles	*I Want to Hold Your Hand* (1963)
Hoagy Carmichael	*The Nearness of You* (1938)
Antonio Vivaldi	Lute Concerto in D major, RV 93 (c. 1730)
J.S. Bach	Lute Suite No. 3 in G minor, BWV 995 (1727)
George M. Cohan	*Give My Regards to Broadway.* (1904)
Irving Berlin	*Alexander's Ragtime Band* (1911)
N. Bayes & J. Norworth	*Shine on Harvest Moon* (1908)

EXERCISES (in lieu of VIEWING GUIDE)

For Unit 1, there are four Listening Exercises (rather than a Viewing Guide). These now follow.

LISTENING EXERCISE 1
LEARNING TO LISTEN IN CONTEXT

In this exercise, you will get practice putting a "context" around the music you know and like. You will do this simply by *asking questions* about music that you ordinarily would simply listen to and enjoy.

1. Select *two* of your favorite songs or pieces of music. They can be any style or type of music. From now on, we will refer to these as "pieces" since not all pieces are songs . . . but all songs are pieces!

2. Now, imagine you are leaving a description of this piece to be included in a time capsule. How would you describe this music to someone who had never heard it? What would you say?

3. After thinking about this, write a paragraph describing each piece: why you liked it, why it was (or wasn't!) really popular, etc. This will be tricky: you may be tempted just to toss in a recording for these future people to hear for themselves! But wait! If *you* were opening a time capsule from a century ago, there's a good chance that neither you, nor anyone you know, would have the ability to play a 78-RPM gramophone recording that was 100 years old. So, try to do it in words.

Consider some of these points while writing your paragraph for each song:

- What kinds of non-musical elements would help a future-listener to appreciate the song the way you do? (say something about history, politics, pop culture, media).
- What would the future listener need to know about contemporary life to appreciate this music: social situations, political events, styles of dance, styles of worship, popular movies or television shows, etc?
- Is the piece you like generally popular, or just one of your favorites? Why or why not? What does that say about you as an individual?
- Where do you listen to this music? On what technology? Where is it designed to be heard? Describe those environments.
- What are you "supposed" to be doing while listening to this music? For instance, if you've selected an up-beat, pop dance tune, you might mention that many people like to listen to it while "working out." Be sure to explain to someone (a century now) what "working out" means! And what does the popularity of "working out" say about our culture?

Title and Artist, Piece No. 1 _____
Your Paragraph:

Title and Artist, Piece No. 2 _____
Your Paragraph:

LISTENING EXERCISE 2
I HEAR MUSIC: A LISTENING DIARY

Step 1. Choose two days in which to fill out the listening diary. Pick two days when you're likely to be out and about.   If possible, pick two consecutive days. Add more "rows" to the charts if you need them.

Step 2. Estimate how many times you think you are likely to hear music during the selected day. Try to foresee the circumstances.

Step 3. Record every time you hear music of any kind. Use the sample chart below to get started. Either fill out the chart as the day goes on, or make notes and fill it out at the end of the day. Try to make the information as complete as possible. Make certain you record whether the "music" was heard voluntarily or involuntarily (if you prefer, use the terms *passive* and *active*).

Step 4. In essay or chart form, analyze what role music has played in the day's routine. How much of the "hearing" was voluntary and how much was involuntary? What was its affect? Was any of the music annoying or pleasing? Was there music you wouldn't have noticed had you not been conducting this survey?

SAMPLE CHART

NATURE OF MUSIC	WHEN/WHERE HEARD	METHOD OF DELIVERY	VOLUNTARY OR INVOLUNTARY	AFFECT ON YOU?
1/3 of a pop song	Monday morning, through the wall of my sister's room before breakfast	Electronic: radio	Involuntary (passive)	Annoying
Some kind of fancy, quiet classical music	Monday, lunchtime, while I was on hold with T-Mobile trying to ask a question about my cell phone	Electronic: Cell phone	Involuntary (passive)	Kind of pretty at first, but then I was frustrated hearing it, because I waited so long.
Songs from *High School Musical* show	Monday afternoon, on school bus while we were coming back from our volleyball game	Live (I'm not sure I'd call it a performance, but it was fun!)	Voluntary (active)	Drove the bus driver crazy.

MY LISTENING DIARY, DAY 1: _____ (date)

I EXPECT TO HEAR MUSIC _____ TIMES TODAY

NATURE OF MUSIC	WHEN./WHERE HEARD	METHOD OF DELIVERY	VOLUNTARY OR INVOLUNTARY	AFFECT ON YOU?

MY LISTENING DIARY, DAY 2: _____ (date)

I EXPECT TO HEAR MUSIC _____ TIMES TODAY

NATURE OF MUSIC	WHEN./WHERE HEARD	METHOD OF DELIVERY	VOLUNTARY OR INVOLUNTARY	AFFECT ON YOU?

LISTENING EXERCISE 3
LISTENING ANALYTICALLY: NEW WAYS TO APPROACH SONGS

Directions: Choose three different songs. They can be familiar songs, or new, or some of each. They can be in any style: Country-Western, Show Music, Pop or Rock, Contemporary Christian, a song from a film, an older song of any style. Or, you can choose pieces from your Listening Set.

Make sure you have the whole song available. A "clip" off the web or brief clip off of a soundtrack will not work as well, as you have no idea "where" you are in the song.

Select one section from each song to focus on: the opening, middle, or final section. This section should be between 1-2 minutes long.   Listen repeatedly and carefully to each chosen section, focusing each time on one of the different musical qualities listed below.

You may answer in any order you like. However, you will probably find it easiest to observe these elements in the order given.

Warning! Do not stop at the first quick answer that pops into your head. Instead, be as distinct and descriptive as possible. You may find this is difficult to do at first, but be patient. Remember that developing listening skills is a fine art, and will serve you well in *many* different areas.

Tempo: How do you describe the tempo (speed) in this section? After your initial response ("fast" or "slow" isn't enough!), try your new Italian terms (*allegro, andante, presto*, etc.). Is the tempo steady, or does it change? Is the tempo an important factor shaping the way the piece sounds? In other words: would the song have a different mood or affect if the tempo were very different?

Dynamics: What is the overriding dynamic level (volume) in this section? *Forte*? *Piano*? Somewhere in the middle (*mezzo piano/mezzo forte*)? Does the dynamic level change? Does the dynamic level help to shape the piece, or is the piece "simply there"?

Instrumentation: To the best of your ability to distinguish them, what instruments are playing in the section? If this is a vocal work (with a sung text), are the instruments simply part of a general background, supporting the vocal line, or does any one instrument specially interact with the vocal melody? To put it another way, does any instrument function as a solo instrument? *You may need to turn up the volume: professionally recorded music is often "mixed" to blend instruments together.*

Surface Rhythm: Describe the surface rhythm. Is the music characterized by quickly moving notes (fast surface rhythm), or are the notes longer, more sustained, and drawn out, with fewer notes passing by.

Texture: Texture is the "thickness" or "thinness" of the music (like a plain hamburger compared to one with layers of cheese, pickles, and lettuce!). How many instruments or vocal melodies are going on? How busy is it "inside" of the music? In this section of the song, how thick or thin is the texture?

Text: If the song has words (lyrics), how much do the words influence the overall affect the music? If the words were absent, would you still get the same feeling from this section of the music?

Harmonic Rhythm: To the best of your ability, analyze how quickly or slowly the chords or harmonies are changing. It may be easy to do this, depending on your experience with music and the simplicity of the song(s) you have chosen. Or it may be challenging, and take repeated listening. Still, give it a try.

Song No. 1 (name):

TEMPO
DYNAMICS
INSTRUMENTATION
SURFACE RHYTHM
TEXTURE
HARMONIC RHYTHM
TEXT

Song No. 2 (name):

TEMPO
DYNAMICS
INSTRUMENTATION
SURFACE RHYTHM
TEXTURE
HARMONIC RHYTHM
TEXT

Song No. 3 (name):

TEMPO
DYNAMICS
INSTRUMENTATION
SURFACE RHYTHM
TEXTURE
HARMONIC RHYTHM
TEXT

DISCUSSION QUESTION: When you've finished evaluating all three selections, write a short essay of three to four paragraphs describing the experience of listening specifically for *these* musical elements. How does this process differ from listening, in general, to music? Can you describe the differences? Does such listening add to, change, enhance, or (perhaps even) limit your appreciation of the song?

LISTENING EXERCISE 4
ACROSS THE GENERATIONS: HEARING A SONG WITH NEW (OLD!) EARS

Step 1. Ask a person one or two generations *older* than you to suggest a favorite piece of music from his or her "youth" (teenage years or the years right out of high school).

Step 2. Get hold of a recording of this music. You may be able to borrow it or use the services of your public library's music holdings, interlibrary loan (audio media usually can be ordered interlibrary-loan), Internet resources like iTunes or Amazon.com.

Step 3. Listen to the piece two or three times. Record your initial response as to the melody, rhythm, instrumentation, text, and overall expression on Part A of the form.

Step 4. Return to the person who suggested it to you. Ask some or all of the questions in Part B of the questionnaire.

Step 5. Compare the two responses—yours and the person for whom this music has special meaning.

Step 6. Write a c. 300-word essay explaining how your sense of the music changed when hearing about it *via* your recommender's memories.

If possible, share your essay with the person who recommended the song to you!

Worksheet
Song title: _____
Artist: _____
Year: _____

Part A. Your initial response

Tempo: 1   2   3   4   5   6   7
                 slow   medium   fast

Overall Energy: 1   2   3   4   5   6   7
                 relaxed   medium   energetic

Predominant dynamic range: soft / medium / loud

Vocal: one singer / duet / vocal group / instrumental only

Subject of text (if there is a text):

Predominant musical element(s)
        Particular instruments heard:
        Interesting harmonies:
        Strong percussion:
        Prominent melody:
        Distinctive rhythm:
        Memorable text:
        Particular atmosphere:

Good dance tune?   yes   no

Good tune for listening, rather than for dancing?   yes   no

Your overall reaction to the song:

Part B.   Questions for the person who recommended the tune

Name of recommender:

Relationship to you (relative, friend, acquaintance, etc.):

When and where did you get to know this song/piece of music?

What were you doing at that time?

Did you know the artist(s) from another tune, or was this completely new to you?

Did you dance to this music?

Did you own a recording of this music? Do you still have it?

Did you keep your interest in the artist(s) and enjoy or even buy other music by him/her/them?

Did you ever see the performer(s) live in some kind of concert? If so, can you describe it?

Do you associate this music with someone or something specific in your life? A friend? A romantic interest? A family member? A favorite location or vacation spot?

Can you describe the memories this music brings back to you?

Do you have a funny or sentimental story or event associated with this music?

Why do you think you really liked this music back then?

When you listen to this music today, does it still strike you the same way?

UNIT 2

MUSIC ENTWINED WITH GREAT EVENTS IN WESTERN HISTORY

FIGURES

Pythagoras
(c. 570-490 BC)

Pope Gregory
(c.540-604 AD)

Johannes Gutenberg
(c. 1400-1468 AD)

Martin Luther
(1483-1546)

*John Wycliffe
(1324-1384)

Johannes Kepler
(1571-1630)

Galileo Galilei
(1564-1642)

PLACES

Trent (Trento), Italy
Eisenach, Germany
Mainz, Germany
Wittenberg, Germany
Wartburg Castle

VOCABULARY

Gregorian Chant
Also known as "plainsong," this simple style of singing accounts for almost all surviving examples of written music from the early Medieval period. It was used in church for worship, and was sung without instrumental accompaniment (*a capella*). This music was named "Gregorian" for Pope Gregory, who was one of the first to insist upon and provide for writing down music. "Chants" are almost always sung in Latin and performed by the church's choir rather than the congregation.

Manuscript (*manus*=hand) + (*scriptum*=writing)
This Latin derivative describes the state and method of preserving information prior to the invention of Gutenberg's printing press. An entire category of people— mostly monks—were specifically trained as copyists to serve in *scriptoria*, special workspaces set aside for the painstaking work of copying *manuscripts*.

Notation
A general term to describe the system and process of writing down musical sounds, or notes. Initially, all notation was hand written (in *manuscript*). Later musical notation was carved into intricate wooden blocks that could be inked (wood-block print). After the invention of the printing press, symbols for notes were set using tiny pieces of metal type (moveable type). Musical notation is more complicated to print than words because there are so many symbols.

Moveable Type
This method of printing enabled the printer to mix and match small pieces of type for text (both letters and numbers) to create words and sentences. As a result, printing became more flexible, faster, and less costly.

Engraving
Originally developed by mapmakers, engraving is the practice of carving any image one wishes to into soft metal plates. The carving, or scoring, of the plate must be done right-to-left, and "backwards" (as in a mirror-image). The plates are then inked and pressed onto parchment or paper. Engraving was especially helpful in printing images involving symbols or designs, such as maps, illustrations, or a musical score!

Lithography
Similar to engraving, except that images are etched into the plates by chemicals rather than metal tools. This resulted in a less expensive method of printing. Lithography was popular in the United States starting in the 19ᵗʰ century.

Reformation/Counter-Reformation
The Reformation was begun by Martin Luther in an attempt to "reform" what he considered to be excesses in the Catholic Church (Western Christian Church). The

church responded by launching the Counter-Reformation, in an attempt to combat the excesses of Luther's followers, or "Lutherans." Although these two movements initially centered around religious matters, the close relationship between the church and government in the 16th century meant that these conflicts became politicized.

Excommunication

The practice of withholding Communion (The Lord's Supper) to church members who have not reconciled themselves to the Church's teaching, and purposefully have chosen to live in opposition to church doctrine.

Hymn

Although songs of praise were used as far back as Old Testament times, hymns became especially important in Lutheran and Protestant worship starting in the 16th century. A new-style hymn was perceived as a simpler, more accessible alternative to Catholic plainchant (Gregorian Chant). The tunes for these hymns were simple, often folk tunes, and each stanza of text reused the same tune. Also, while chants were typically sung in Latin, hymns were in the "vernacular" – the local language. Thus the Germans sang hymns in German, while the Dutch sang them in Dutch, etc.

Cantata

A dramatic work for voice(s) and instruments that conveys a story or theme. Cantatas were not staged or acted; rather, they had various purposes, including serving as vivid musical illustrations of the theme of the worship service. The new Protestant churches in particular embraced the Cantata for use in their services.

Gramophone

The gramophone was the earliest successful device invented to record and replay sound. Thomas Edison gets the credit for the invention (1877), although other inventors were working on similar devices in that same period. While envisioned as a device to record and preserve speech (and the voices of famous people), the gramophone became the new way to preserve and transmit music. In turn, it changed the dynamics of music-making forever because it gave the public access to music even when live performances were not available. Music no longer was constrained to real time (heard at the same time it was performed).

Tin Pan Alley

The space between West 28th Street and Fifth and Sixth Avenues in New York City, where dozens of music publishing houses were located as early as the 1880s. Hoping to convince a publisher to buy a song, songwriters would "pound out" tunes on pianos, either singing them or bringing a singer along to do so. If the song pleased, then it would be published. The sound of all these pianos flowed out the windows to create a cacophony best described as rattling tin pans—hence the name Tin Pan Alley.

Acoustics

The scientific study of sound and hearing. Sound is a quantifiable scientific property, governed by certain physical laws that can be studied, and even manipulated by outside forces to achieve a certain desired result.

DATES:

1440:   First printing press invented by goldsmith Johannes Gutenberg in Mainz, Germany.

1517:   On October 31, Martin Luther nailed his 95 Theses (objections against church practices) to a side door of the cathedral in the German town of Wittenberg, inadvertently beginning a reaction that resulted in the Protestant Reformation.

1545:   Council of Trent. A series of meetings held by the Catholic Church to make reforms and to counter the growing appeal of the new Protestants.

1587:   Sir Walter Raleigh's third expedition to North America sets out to establish a new colony at Roanoke (an island off the coast of Virginia).

1607:   Jamestown Settlement founded in what is now Virginia by the English "Virginia Company."

1618-1648:   Thirty Years' War. A series of bloody religious conflicts to determine whether Europe would be a Catholic or Protestant region. Ultimately, little was solved, and the northern part of Europe (today's Scandinavia, The Netherlands, Northern Germany) remained predominantly Protestant, while the southern part (today's Austria, Italy, Switzerland, Southern Germany) remained primarily Catholic. Europeans still speak about the horror of this war, despite the centuries that have passed.

1620:   Plymouth Colony, near Plymouth, Massachusetts, founded by the Pilgrims.

1666:   A Royal Academy of Sciences is established by Louis XIV, showing his wholehearted support of modern (and often controversial) scientific research.

1682:   William Penn founds Pennsylvania as a refuge for Quakers.

1929- 1939:   The Great Depression, originating in the United States, but with parallels in Europe. Ultimately it is the preparation for, and execution of, World War II that brings an end to the economic hardships.

LISTENING

Gabrieli   **Canzon septimi toni, a 8 (No. 2)** *In Ecclesiis* (CD1/tr3)

Mouret   **Rondeau** (CD1/tr4)

WEBSITES

http://www.ideafinder.com/history/inventors/gutenberg.htm
A basic biographical outline of Johannes Gutenberg and a historical narrative of his invention of the printing press.

http://www.greatsite.com/timeline-english-bible-history/martin-luther.html
Although this website offers a wealth of information regarding church and Christian history, and the history of Bible translation, it also gives a great biographical sketch of Martin Luther. You will want to examine carefully the sections that tell the story of his time at the Wartburg Castle, his own writings on the Bible, and his complex opinion on the relationship between Judaism and Scripture.

You will want to examine the other tabs on this site, including "Ancient Rare Bibles and Books" and "Facsimile Reproductions." Also, after reading about Luther, click on the links to information on John Wycliffe, John Hus, Thomas Linacre, and John Colet.

http://www.timelineindex.com/content/view/546
After examining several of the links on the left-hand side of the site that apply to this unit (including "Reformation" and "16th Century"), scroll down to examine the section dealing with the Council of Trent and John Calvin.

http://www.bl.uk/treasures/gutenberg/homepage.html
Online access to the British Library's copies of the Gutenberg Bible, including a "Background" section, which deals with the technical side of the printing process and the other texts Gutenberg printed, plus a "Texts" section that will allow you to

look up-close at two copies. Examine the "Basics" section first, which may be the information that younger students will find most helpful.

http://www.music-for-church-choirs.com/gregorian-chant.html
http://www.music-for-church-choirs.com/hymns.html

This site will give you a thorough overview of both Gregorian Chant and Hymns. If you are a fan of choirs, or sing in a choir (especially a church choir), you will find a number of the links interesting and informative.

http://www.suite101.com/lesson.cfm/17556/939/5

An incredibly valuable site for scientific information, the eight lessons on the historical development of science and the modern scientific method offer a fascinating outline of the scientific revolution, from Columbus to Newton. Lesson 6 deals with the development of the French Royal Academy, but you will want to examine all six of the lessons.

NOTE: Because of the limited timeframe covered, the issues of Intelligent Design, creationism, evolution, etc., are not addressed in any way.

http://www.academie-sciences.fr/presentation/historique_gb.htm

This is the official website of the *Institut de France Académie des Sciences*. This particular link will take you to an English-language presentation of the history of the Academy. Older students may wish to examine the other links to the Academy's archives, publications, or foundations.

http://www.historylearningsite.co.uk/thirty_years_war.htm

As you will quickly deduce from this site, the Thirty Years' War was in fact a long series of conflicts, treaties, and broken promises. For older students, the links on this page will offer a veritable semester's worth of European history study; you will want to become familiar with this site for use in your history studies. Younger students may prefer to examine the links one at a time.

http://www.hyperhistory.com/online_n2/civil_n2/hist_6.html

True to its name, this site offers a stunning assortment of links, organized in an all-inclusive (but slightly overwhelming!) timeline that covers people, places, things, ideas, and historical epochs. To access information on the Thirty Years' War quickly, go to **http://www.hyperhistory.com/online_n2/civil_n2/histscript6_n2/thirty1.html**. From there, you can choose to click on the "People" link, that will take you to a timeline based upon individuals, or click on "History," which will take you to the main page.

http://www.acoustics.org/

The official website of the Acoustical Society of America, this site is a valuable resource for fundamental explanations of acoustical properties. You will also wish to visit **http://paws.kettering.edu/~drussell/demos.html**, which offers fantastic animated explanations that demonstrate these properties. Be sure to scroll down and pay special attention to the section on "Room Acoustics."

PUTTING IT ALL TOGETHER:

1. Regardless of your religion or religious affiliation, you should be aware of the tremendous role the Bible has played in the development of Western culture. Why do you think Gutenberg chose the Bible as his first major printing project? How was this Bible crucial to the development of the new industry of printing? Also, do a little research on the history of the English translation of the Bible.

2. Was the Council of Trent the first "council" to be held by the Roman Catholic church? If not, why was it considered one of the most important? What was the *Index Liborum Prohibitorum*? What kinds of things were on it? What topics?

3. Do a Google search on "Gutenberg." What is "Project Gutenberg"? Do you think Gutenberg would have approved?

4. After you have examined the websites for the French *Académie des Sciences*, do a Google search on "Royal Academy of Sciences." What do you notice? What do these sites tell you about the priority of these nations? Why are they all "Royal"? Select a few sites for countries that you are interested in: how are they similar to the French *Académie*? What differences do you notice?

5. Luther's translation of the Bible into German was both a challenge to the authority of the Catholic Church and an important step in the standardization of the German language. How do you think this standardization contributed to the Thirty Years' War? What other impact did Luther's translation have on German culture?

6. Research the development of the radio. Try to determine how quickly radio went from an invention to an indispensible part of daily life. Seek statistics that document the economic impact of radio on the music industry and on advertising. Also, who were the first "stars" on the radio? Try, too, to find statistics indicating the present status of radio within the entertainment industry.

VIEWING GUIDE

1. The rise of radio in the _____ (decade) changed the popular music industry because _____ _____. The Internet has caused another set of changes, particularly because _____.

2. One of the most important technological innovations in Western history came with the invention of the _____ in _____ (place) by _____ (person). Books were printed on both _____ and _____.

3. The _____ actually first used the idea of printing with moveable type (both ceramic and wood).

4. Before the invention of the printing press, how were "books" produced? _____ _____ _____.

5. Parchment is actually made of _____! Gutenberg used both parchment and paper: about _____ sheep were needed for each of the 35 parchment copies of Gutenberg's Bible.

6. Scholars estimate that, prior to Gutenberg, there were about _____ hand-copied books in Europe. Within fifty years, more than _____ books were circulating.

7. How was music reproduced in the Medieval period? _____ _____.

8. Did anything in the earliest musical notation indicate whether the notes were long or short in duration (length)? Yes No

9. During the 16th century, printers started to use the process of engraving, which was first developed by _____.

10. The difficult thing about engraving is that every image must be etched (how?)_____!

11. _____, called "the poor man's engraving," used chemicals.

12. How did the gramophone affect popular music, including the sale of printed music? _____ _____ .

13. In what American city do you find Tin Pan Alley? _____ What commercial activity went on there? _____ _____

14. How did Tin Pan Alley get its name? _____ _____ _____ .

15. Using the science of _____, we can analyze and explain every sound in the universe!

16. Modern acoustical understanding was based on the work of early Greek mathematician _____, and then it was picked up by Greek philosopher _____ .

17. Architecture and acoustics have been intertwined for centuries, for example _____ _____ .

18. _____ (nationality) King Louis XIV was a powerful European monarch. A modern thinker, he used the _____ as his symbol, connecting him to _____ .

19. Scientists examining the relationship of the planets and sun during this era included _____ and _____ .

20. The age known as the _____ was characterized by scientific achievement and the collecting of knowledge. Artists and thinkers in the following century were more concerned with _____ _____ .

UNIT 3

TECHNOLOGY, TERMINOLOGY, AND CULTURAL PERSPECTIVE

VOCABULARY

Genre
From the Latin *genus*, for birth, family, or nation. In music, *genre* means the type, kind, or category of music, referring to its function and form. Genres include symphony, opera, oratorio, cantata, ballet, tone poem, character piece, and dance.

Symphony
A piece of music written for a large group of instruments (usually an orchestra). It is generally divided into multiple, distinct sections called *movements*. Remember: an orchestra is the group that *plays* the music. A symphony is a genre or type of music. You will find orchestras with the word "symphony" in their title, such as the London Symphony Orchestra or the Chicago Symphony Orchestra.

Quartet
A genre of music played by four players, usually strings (two violins, one viola, and one cello), but any combination of four players (or singers) makes up a quartet.

Opera
A story presented by singers on a stage. Performances involve singing, acting, costumes, lights, and staging. Thus, operas are referred to as being "staged."

Concerto
From the Italian verb *concertare*, meaning to agree or to harmonize. Music for this genre usually involves a soloist (sometimes a small group acting as a "soloist" together) playing in some kind of musical conversation with a larger group.

Movements
The divisions of a musical composition. Movements usually have a distinct beginning and ending (sometimes making them seem like separate, individual pieces). Here's an analogy: a textbook (like a composition) consists of separate chapters (or movements). Each chapter can have sub-divisions (or sections).

Virtuoso (plural Virtuosi or Virtuosos)
An extraordinarily gifted or capable performer. The incredibly difficult music virtuosi play is referred to as "virtuosic," and often has been composed simply to show off the performer's exceptional ability, or virtuosity.

Tempo

Literally, this word is Italian for "time." This term is used to refer to the speed of music. You can describe *tempo* with the following terms (all are Italian):

Presto, or "quick"

Vivo, or "lively," from the Latin verb *vivere*, to live

Andante, literally, "to go," from the verb *andare*. Be careful! Sometimes this term is inaccurately described as "slow." But think of all the different speeds people use to "go": if you have a little brother or sister, you know how fast (or slow) "go" can be!

Allegro, or "happy" and, thus, a moderately quick tempo

Adagio, or "at ease" and, thus, a slow tempo (slower than Andante)

Largo, or "broadly" and, thus, a slow tempo (slower than Andante)

Molto/Meno

Italian for "very much" and "less." These are "flavoring" words, which can be added as adjectives to other terms.

Ensemble

From the Latin root *insimul*, meaning "simultaneous" or "at the same time."

LISTENING

George Handel	Courante from Suite No. 8 in F minor, HWV 441 (1720)
Joseph Haydn	***Allegro* from Trumpet Concerto in E-flat major, HOB VIIe:1** (CD1/tr19)
	Symphony No. 94 in G major ("Surprise") (1792)
Wolfgang Mozart	Papagena! Papagena! Papagena! Act II, Scene VI, *The Magic Flute* (*Die Zauberflöte*), K. 620 (1791)
Ludwig van Beethoven	***Allegro scherzando* from Concerto No. 1 in C major, Op. 15 (1797)** (CD2/tr5)

Andante espressivo from Sonata No. 26 in E-flat major ("*Les Adieux*"), Op. 81a (c.1809)

Presto agitato from Sonata No. 14 in C-sharp minor ("Moonlight" or *Quasi una fantasia*), Op. 27 No. 2 (1801)

Carl Maria von Weber

Invitation to the Dance, Op. 65 (1811)

Franz Schubert

Waltz No. 14 in F minor, Op. 33, D. 783 (1824))

Frederic Chopin

March (*Marche funèbre*): Lento from Sonata No. 2 in B minor, Op. 35 (1839)

Waltz in D-flat major, Op. 64, no. 1 (1847)

Edvard Grieg

Piano Concerto in A minor, Op. 16 (1869)

Johann Strauss II

Blue Danube Waltz, Op. 314 (1866)

Peter Tchaikovsky

Waltz from Act I, *Swan Lake*, Op. 20 (1876)

Piano Concerto No. 1 in B-flat major, Op. 23 (1875)

Giacomo Puccini

Musette's Waltz (*Quando me'n vo*) from Act II, *La Boheme* (1896)

Tomaso Albinoni

Adagio in G minor for Strings and Organ Continuo (originally thought to be a reconstructed Baroque composition, but revealed to be composed in 1958 by Remo Giazotto)

Bill Haley and the Comets

Rock Around the Clock (1955)

Andrew Lloyd Webber

"Music of the Night" *Phantom of the Opera* (1986)

PUTTING IT ALL TOGETHER

1.   Carefully study and memorize the terms for tempo in this unit. Think of a specific thing or activity that each Italian term for tempo (speed) represents to you; you could even find a picture for each in a newspaper or a magazine. Make

flashcards or a collage of these images and terms and keep them handy for future reference.

2.   Go to the following website and get acquainted with the main types and sizes of musical ensembles in both classical Western and Eastern music:

http://www.bambooweb.com/articles/m/u/Musical_ensemble.html

Be able to answer the following questions:

* What are vocal ensembles called?
* Are there any ensembles in which instruments and voices are mixed?
* What is the difference between an "orchestra" and a "string orchestra"?
* What is the difference between an "orchestra" and a "chamber orchestra"?
* What are the families of instruments within the orchestra?
* Which instruments belong to which families?

3.   If you are unfamiliar with the instruments used in Western music (violins, oboes, trumpets, bassoons, tubas, timpani, etc.), spend some time in this unit becoming acquainted with them. You can find lots of material by searching in your local library or online. A few good places to start are:

http://www.dsokids.com/listen/instrumentlist.aspx
http://library.thinkquest.org/11315/instrum.htm

4.   Older students may want to spend some time researching the investment of time and money that goes into the purchase of some of these instruments. Click on the categories and see what instruments come up. What family of instruments, in general, is the most costly? Why? How (and where) are instruments made? What family of instruments will last for the longest number of years? The shortest?

VIEWING GUIDE

1.   Talking about form really means discussing the _____ of something.

2.   Form is all around us, and easy to see in things like (examples) _____ _____.

3.   "Movements" are _____.

4.   Where are tempo markings usually located on the page of a musical score? _____.

5.   *Allegro* means _____.

6.   *Andante* means _____.

7.   *Adagio* and *largo* have similar (but not identical) meanings. *Adagio* means _____, and *largo* means _____.

8.   *Presto* means _____, and *vivo* comes from the Latin verb _____, and means "quickly."

9.   _____ and _____ mean "less" and "more."

10.   Did composers always indicate tempo markings? _____. Justify your answer. _____ _____.

11.   We can compare the talents and skills of a virtuoso performer to _____.

12.   Understanding _____ is the key to music-making.

13.   *Genre* means a _____.

14.   Giving specific names to genres and styles can get confusing because _____ _____.

15.   A symphony is usually written for a (size) _____ group of instruments.

16.   Is a quartet always played by stringed instruments like violins, violas, and cellos? _____

17.   The basic idea of opera goes back to the _____.

18.   "Concerto" comes from the Italian verb *concertare*, which means _____.

19.   How large is an ensemble? Does it have a set size? Has it been the same size throughout music history? (explain) _____ _____.

UNIT 4

FANFARE AND POWER:
THE COURT OF LOUIS XIV

FIGURES
Louis XIV
(1638-1715)

Jean-Baptiste Lully
(1632-1687)

Charles le Brun
(1619-1690)

Johannes Kepler
(1571-1630)

Galileo Galilei
(1564-1642)

William Harvey
(1578-1657)

Molière (stage name of Jean-Baptiste Poquelin)
(1622-1673)

Marc-Antoine Charpentier
(1643-1704)

PLACES

Paris, France
Versailles, France

VOCABULARY

Versailles
Originally a hunting *château*, Versailles was built into Europe's greatest show palace. Nearly every other European monarchy modeled its palaces after Versailles, borrowing its architecture, landscaping, and fountains as the ultimate model of imperial power demonstrated by human design.

Court
This general word can actually apply to a number of things. The "court" can refer to a physical location, as in being "at court." It can also refer to the group of people who were gathered around a monarch, as in being a "member of the court" of Louis XIV.

Château
In French, literally, "house"; a term usually referring to great houses built in the country. Though not intended to be palaces, these houses had to be large enough for the noble family, their court, and their employees. As a result, they can be as large (and grand) as a palace.

Fête
In French: party, festival, or birthday. This word is used to indicate celebrations; if you wish someone "Happy Birthday" in French, you will say, *"Bonne fête."*

Divertissement
In French, literally, a diversion or light entertainment. A *divertissement* is usually a short musical piece, often for dancing, that was intended to be an interlude during breaks in a larger, longer performance. These were a sort of live "commercial break," without advertising any product for sale.

Faux pas
In French, literally, "false step."

Dauphin
The title given to the son of a French monarch (usually the oldest son) who was the intended heir to the throne. Although we usually think of such an individual as a "prince," many monarchies (and many languages) use a specific term to refer to the next king, separating him from the other "ordinary" princes.

Salle
In French, a large hall or auditorium. The Hall of Mirrors is called *Salle des glaces.* Compare *glaces* with glaze and glass.

Maître de musique
French for "master of music," usually an official title conferred by a king to one composer in a supervisory position.

Overture
A composition for instruments only. It serves as an introduction to a longer work such as the opening for a ballet or opera. It comes from the French verb *ouvrir*, to open. Usually, an overture is very catchy and fun to listen to, sometimes offering shortened versions of the melodies to follow. Overtures originally had a practical purpose: before it became customary in the late 19th century to lower the house lights, an overture alerted the audience that the performance was about to begin.

Männerchor (*Männer*= men) + (*Chor*=choir)
In German, a choir of male singers. It is a long-standing tradition in German folk music. Even today, small villages will boast a very proficient men's choir.

Kapellmeister (*Kapelle*= Chapel) + (*Meister*=master)
In German, the "master of the chapel," who was responsible for composing and/or directing musical performances in the chapel and, by extension, the entire court.

Fasching
In German, this is another word for Carnival, the unofficial season of feasting and parties that leads up to Lent.

Les Vingt-quatre Violons du Roi
In French, "The twenty-four violins of the King," a carefully trained string ensemble conducted by Lully during his service to Louis XIV.

DATES

1610:	Santa Fe established as the capital of New Mexico
1630-1643:	English Puritans immigrate to the Massachusetts Bay colony.
1661:	**Louis XIV becomes king, establishes Versailles as his main residence.**
1664:	New Amsterdam becomes "New York."
1670:	Hudson's Bay Company chartered.

LISTENING

Jean-Joseph Mouret	**Rondeau for trumpet and organ (1729)** (CD1/tr4)
Marc-Antoine Charpentier	**Sanctus and Benedictus from *Messe di Minuet pour Nöel*, H. 9 (1690)** (CD1/tr7)
	Noel: Un flambeau, Janette, Isabelle, H. 460c
Jean-Baptiste Lully	*Te Deum* H. 146 **Ouverture: Ballet d'Alcidiane et Polexandere** (CD1/tr5)
	Bourrée pour les Basques, from *Ballet de Xerxes* (CD1/tr6)
Jeremiah Clarke	Trumpet Voluntary in D major (or, "Prince of Denmark's March," formerly attributed to Henry Purcell) (c.1699)
Joan Baptista Cabanilles (1644-1712)	Music for the Spanish court, including *Tientos, Passacalles,* and dances like *Gallardas*
	DVD Performance. The Art of Baroque Dance: Folies d'Espagne From Page to Stage, directed by Carol Teten (2006)

WEBSITES

http://www.louis-xiv.de/

This website is a great "first stop" on your journey to learning about the life and times of Louis XIV. You will even find video games about Versailles.
Note: Some allusions are made to Louis' unchaste lifestyle.

http://history.hanover.edu/texts/louisxiv.html

On this site you will find two contemporary descriptions of Louis and life at his court. Younger students may find the style of writing difficult to negotiate, but the second excerpt gives a detailed account of a typical evening at the court of Versailles.

http://www.chateauversailles.fr/homepage

The official homepage of Versailles, you can use this site to practice your French or hit the "Française" button for the English option. Because Versailles is now a state-owned museum, there will be a number of temporary exhibits being shown at any given time. It's worthwhile to bookmark the site and return to it again in the future. This website will be helpful when studying any of the French kings *after* Louis XIV.

http://www.versailles-tourisme.com/en/discoveries/history.html

If you are interested in the history of Versailles before its royal development, this site is a good place to start. You will discover that Versailles had a very long and grand life, dating back in records as far as 1038 AD. You will certainly want to explore the many links to music, culture, architecture, and theater at Versailles.

http://www.historyteacher.net/APEuroCourse/WebLinks/WebLinks-AgeOfAbsolutism.htm

This site offers a long list of links related to the general topic "Age of Absolutism." While some of them do not deal directly with Louis XIV or French History, you can easily determine from scanning the page which ones you are most interested in for this particular unit; you will probably want to bookmark this for future reference. Older students will want to examine the primary source material, as well as the general course of study laid out on a different page. It can be accessed by clicking on "Topics" at the bottom of the above link, or by going to:
http://www.historyteacher.net/APEuroCourse/Topics/TOPIC-AgeOfAbsolutism.htm

http://www.nea.gov/

The official homepage of the National Endowment for the Arts offers a helpful overview of the organization by following the "National Council for the Arts" link, under the "About Us" banner. Although the links offering instructions on participation in grants and partnerships are not for general reading, you will want to spend lots of time in the Audio and Video section. Also, click on "NEA Spotlight" under the banner "Features" to get an idea of some of the NEA's most recently-funded projects.

http://www.whitehousehistory.org/index.html

A fascinating online look into the White House, this site is maintained by the White House Historical Association and offers a number of online exhibits, timelines, information about current White House happenings, and much, much more. For the immediate purposes of this unit, click on "History and New Media," then "Facts and Trivia." You will want to examine all of those links at some point, but go first to "Music and Dance." Though brief, this list will offer a few interesting anecdotes for younger students, or a few topics of further study for older students. Then, click on "Timelines" at the bottom of the page, and scroll down to select "Music." Because this topic is organized several decades at a time, you may want to return to this location several times during future units to remember what was going on in the

White House at any given time. Finally, scroll down from "Music" to the timeline for "Musical Performances."

http://www.naxos.com/composerinfo/Jean_Baptiste_Lully/22610.htm
A valuable website that offers pictures and a brief biography of Lully, along with examples of his compositions.

http://www.johanneskepler.com/
The life and works of Johannes Kepler, including quotes, a list of works, and additional references.

http://www.2020site.org/moliere/
The life, works, and times of Jean-Baptiste Poquelin (Molière), one of the world's great playwrights.

PUTTING IT ALL TOGETHER

1.   Using a combination of the suggested websites and an encyclopedia site, research the history of Versailles' famous Hall of Mirrors. Pay special attention to the events taking place there in 1871 and in 1919. In what condition did the hall (and Versailles in general) survive World War II? Have there been other significant political events there in the twentieth century? Has the hall been renovated recently? How long did this take?

2.   Consider any special music performance spaces in your neighborhood or city. How many are there? Are they used for music only? If not, what other kinds of performances are scheduled? How are they different from Versailles, and why? Many of these places today are called "Performing Arts" centers, and may be very large buildings that house a number of different spaces. If you have access to one of these, arrange a field trip.

3.   One of the music performance spaces in your neighborhood is probably your church or house of worship. Even if the music there is performed only as part of worship services, this is probably the place where you most frequently hear live music. Spend some time interviewing your *Kapellmeister*, or music minister. Explain that you have been thinking more about live musical performances. Tell him or her that you are interested in knowing what kind of decisions and activities take place "behind the scenes," since that person's job is to provide live music on a weekly basis. Some questions you might ask include:

- How did you get this job, and how long have you had it?
- What kind of preparation is required for this sort of job, including education or prior experience?

- What are the most important things that you consider when planning services? How long does this typically take?
- Are there other, non-service, musical performances? Are there rules or policies for these?
- What do you like most about your performance space? What would you like to change?
- Are there others (audio engineers, video engineers, etc.) who are involved in making the music happen?
- How much rehearsal or practice time occurs each week?
- Are extra or guest musicians ever hired?

What are some extra things that the musicians would like, but cannot fit into the budget? Why are they necessary?

4.   Spend some time researching America's National Endowment for the Arts. When was it founded, and by whom? What are the stated purposes of the organization? What are some examples of its most recent projects? Consider carefully the advantages and disadvantages of state-sponsored art: what were some of the pitfalls of "government" (royal) funding for the arts during Louis' day? Do these same challenges still exist, or have modern times brought different, modern, problems?

5.   Louis became king at a very young age; while this may sound like great fun, it actually resulted in lots of difficulty for him. Many of the characteristics of his reign were the result of his attempts to cope with or overcome these difficulties. Using the websites, and perhaps another book or two from your local library, learn as much as you can about Louis' upbringing, early family life, and education. Does this sound like a pleasant way to grow up? Do you think he made good decisions? Why or why not? Does anything about his upbringing surprise you? Which aspects might have made him a better, or worse, ruler?

6.   Although you know how Versailles *became* important, it has mostly retained its status in modern society because of its past glory. When did Versailles lose its place as the center of the French court? Why? To which location was the court transferred? In what ways would these changes have affected other aspects of noble life?

7.   Examine the history of the White House. It is interesting to note that, unlike Versailles, cultural happenings at the White House tend to be a reflection of American culture rather than setting the trend for the rest of the country. Examine the timeline of cultural happenings at the White House. What priorities does this timeline reflect?

VIEWING GUIDE

1.   Three major institutions that have supported art throughout Western Culture: _____ , _____ , and _____ .

2.   What are the differences between *voluntary* and *involuntary* listening experiences? _____
_____ .

3.   For much of Western music history, why were most choirs for "boys only"? _____
_____ .

4.   European monarchs used the court of _____
as their model for power and extravagance both during his lifetime and for centuries afterwards.

5.   A _____ is the head of all of the church music and may also be in charge of an entire court musical establishment.

6.   The _____ was the keyboard instrument of choice in those days, and it fit well with the aristocracy.

7.   In terms of power, we call the 17th and 18th centuries the Age of _____ . Powerful monarchs included _____
_____ .

8.   Although it is huge, Louis XIV's palace of Versailles is called a _____ , which means "house." It was built originally to be a _____ .

9.   During the Age of Absolutism, monarchs would do almost anything to acquire the best _____ .
Why? Because the arts were a symbol of power!

10.   Louis XIV was known as the _____ , which associated him with _____ .

11.   Paintings of Alexander the Great brought attention to a painter named _____ who would become Court Painter.

12.   During this time, scientists were developing a modern understanding of the _____. One of the ways Louis XIV demonstrated his support of the new sciences was to _____.

13.   Louis XIV was a great _____. His courtiers were expected to join in. In his court, a mistaken step, known as a _____, could signal a demotion in a career. As Louis XIV grew older, the dancing masters at court needed to be diplomatic and make sure _____, who no longer could execute the most difficult steps.

14.   Louis XIV also had a great impact on fashion and on technology. His elegant taste is best seen in a grand room called _____. This room was also the site for important events in more recent history, including _____ _____.

15.   The composer Lully teamed up with the great playwright of the era named _____ for some fantastic productions.

16.   Music accompanied everything King Louis XIV did, including _____.

17.   A popular type of music called a _____ is particularly fitting for this period, especially with the grand opening chords and dotted rhythms (long, short-long, short-long).

18.   When you go to visit _____, you'd better set aside at least three days: one for the _____ and two for the _____.

UNIT 5

SWEEPING AWAY THE RENAISSANCE INTO THE BAROQUE

FIGURES

Johann Sebastian Bach
(1685-1750)

Dante Alighieri
(c. 1265-1321)

Giovanni Boccaccio
(1313-1375)

Filippo Brunelleschi
(1377-1446)

Leonardo da Vinci
(1452-1519)

Claudio Monteverdi
(1567-1643)

Giovanni Gabrieli
(1554-1612)

Jean-Philippe Rameau
(1683-1764)

Sir Isaac Newton
(1643-1727)

*Gottfried Leibniz
(1646-1716)

PLACES

Florence, Italy
Venice, Italy
Hamburg, Germany

VOCABULARY

Renaissance
Literally, "re-birth." This term refers to the rebirth of ideas from Classical (Ancient) Greek and Rome within European culture starting mid-14th century.

Recitative
A style of singing used when lots of dialogue or informative text must be related. The text is in prose and is essentially "recited" to music, using a rhythm and style that resembles speech.

Aria
In contrast to recitative, an aria (or "air") is the lyrical portion of an opera, the song-like sections where emotions are expressed using melody. Aria texts usually rhyme.

Prima/Seconda Prattica
A lively debate among composers of Monteverdi's time centered around these two "practices." The "first practice" (*Prima Prattica*), characteristic of pre-Baroque music, emphasized the older and more elaborate (polyphonic) style of composition. The "second practice" (*Seconda Prattica*), in direct contrast, focused on a simplified style that highlighted a single melody called monody.

Monody
A musical style or texture featuring a single line of melody.

Opera
Literally, "work," in Italian. Later, it came to mean a genre featuring a story that is set to music and "staged" with costumes, sets, acting, and even dance.

Toccata
From the Italian *toccare*, meaning "to touch." Composed for keyboard instruments or the lute, this type of instrumental piece was designed to highlight the performer's technical ability—literally, how well the player could "touch" the instrument!

Libretto (plural *Libretti*, Librettos)
The "little book" (from *libro*) that provides the script for an opera or oratorio. The text was printed in small format (hence *libretto*) and sold cheaply to audience members. The libretto shapes the work (remember: *Prima le parole, e dopo la musica*). Throughout much of Western music history, the individual writing the libretto (librettist) had greater status than the composer.

"Lieto Fine"
"Happy ending." Even tragic works during the Baroque period required a *lieto fine*.

Polyphony (*poly*=many) + (*phon*=sound)
This style, or texture, of music features many melodies (each independent) interwoven into one complex musical fabric.

Dissonance/Consonance
Two contrasting words for describing the basic quality of music: music that is "consonant" features sounds that are pleasing, and fit together well. "Dissonant" music is most quickly recognized as clashing combinations of sounds that create tension and a general sense of unrest.

Basso Continuo
Also known as "figured bass," *basso continuo* was a common musical texture in the Baroque era. It requires two parts: an instrument that plays chords or harmonies, like a keyboard or lute, and a low instrument with sustained sound such as bassoon or cello able to produce a bass line as a foundation.

Fantasia
A certain kind of instrumental work that was intended to sound "fantastic." Loosely organized in several sections, a *fantasia* would go from fast to slow, loud to soft, simple to complex, allowing the performer to show off all styles of playing.

Fugue
A very intricate form of polyphony, in which there are a specific number of musical lines or voices (usually four) that all present and develop the same musical idea.

Tragedie lyrique
In French, literally, "lyrical tragedy." This was a French style of courtly operatic drama, somewhat similar to Italian *opera seria*.

DATES

1475:	Famed Renaissance artist Michelangelo is born.
1492:	Christopher Columbus discovers the New World
1505:	Leonardo da Vinci completes the *Mona Lisa.*
1600-1900:	**"Common Practice Era" in Western Music**
1607:	**Premiere of Monteverdi's opera *Orfeo***
1642:	**Premiere of Monteverdi's opera *Coronation of Poppea***

LISTENING

Josquin des Prez	*Missa L'homme armé* (c. 1495)
Clément Jannequin	*Chant des oiseaux* (c.1529)
Gesualdo da Venosa	*Quinto Libro di Madrigali* ("Fifth Book of Madrigals") (1611)
Giovanni Gabrieli	Magnificat a 14 (1615)
Thomas Morley	*Now is the Month of Maying* (Madrigal)
Thomas Weelkes	*As Vesta was from Latmos Hill Descending* (Madrigal) (1601)
John Dowland	***Flow my Tears*** **(c. 1600)** (CD1/tr1)
Claudio Monteverdi	***Toccata*** **from *Orfeo*** **(1609)** (CD1/tr2) Prologue to *Orfeo* Shepherd's Chorus from Act. 1, *Orfeo* *Possente spiritu* from Act 3, *Orfeo* *Lagrime d'amante al sepolcro dell'amata, a 5* (A Lover's Tears at the Tomb of his Beloved) (c. 1614) *Pur ti Miro* from Act 3, *L'incoronazione di Poppea* (1642)
Johann Pachelbel	Canon and Gigue in D major for Three Violins and Basso Continuo (1680)
J.S. Bach	Toccata in G major, BWV 915 (1706) Fugue for Organ in G minor ("Little G minor"), BWV 578 (1707) *St. Mathew Passion*, BWV 244 (1727)
George Handel	"And with His Stripes we are Healed," Chorus from *Messiah*, HWV 56 (1741) "I know that My Redeemer Liveth," Aria from *Messiah*, HWV 56 (1741)

"With Rage I Shall Burst," Aria from *Saul*, HWV 53 (1738)

WEBSITES

http://www.naxos.com/person/Johann_Sebastian_Bach_17648/17648.htm
The official Naxos website on J. S. Bach, including biographical information, images, listening lists, and audio links. Also view:
http://www.naxos.com/catalogue/item.asp?item_code=C49023
http://www.jsbach.org/

http://www.baroquemusic.org/index.html
This beautiful website is full of images and information on the Baroque Era, specifically its music and composers. You will want to spend lots of time at this site, as it includes links to biographical information on many composers as well as more general information on the history and architecture of the period.

http://www.greatdante.net/
An online guide to the life, times, and works of the great Dante.

http://www.historyguide.org/ancient/boccaccio.html
This site offers a brief biographical sketch of Boccaccio and an introduction to his most significant works.

http://www.brown.edu/Departments/Italian_Studies/dweb/index.php
A multimedia guide to Boccaccio's *Decameron*, including links to maps and literary themes, information on The Plague, and the work's socio-historical setting.

http://www.greatbuildings.com/architects/Filippo_Brunelleschi.html
A guide to images and information on Brunelleschi's significant building projects.

http://www.yesnet.yk.ca/schools/projects/renaissance/brunelleschi.html
Biographical information on Brunelleschi, including a narrative of his exceptionally diverse vocational training and how this background helped to make him the "Father of Renaissance Architecture."

http://www.mos.org/sln/Leonardo/

An online portal into the life and times of this great Renaissance thinker and artist, produced by Boston's Museum of Science. Older students will want to view:
http://library.thinkquest.org/3044/
http://www.artcyclopedia.com/artists/leonardo_da_vinci.html

http://www.naxos.com/person/Claudio_Monteverdi/24641.htm
The official Naxos website to Monteverdi, including biographical information, images, listening lists, and audio links. Also visit:
http://www.manteau.de/claudio.html

http://www.naxos.com/person/Giovanni_Gabrieli/27189.htm
The official Naxos website on Gabrieli, including biographical information, images, listening lists, and audio links.

http://www.greatbuildings.com/buildings/St_Marks.html
A guide to the architecture and images of St. Mark's Basilica in Venice, the specific performance space for which Gabrieli prepared his compositions. The site includes a 3D model and a brief commentary on the history of the Basilica.

http://www.naxos.com/composerinfo/Jean_Philippe_Rameau/21006.htm
The official Naxos guide to Rameau, including biographical information, images, listening lists, and audio files.

http://www.ibiblio.org/wm/paint/glo/renaissance/
Although this site is oriented around visual art, it offers a glimpse into the "rebirth" of the arts in different geographical regions of Europe.

http://www.learner.org/interactives/renaissance/
For students of all ages, an interactive guide to the Renaissance, with many links to related resources and hands-on projects as well!

A guide to the instruments of the Baroque era. Older students will wish to visit:
http://www.culturekiosque.com/klassik/features/ra1baroq.htm

http://opera.stanford.edu/
This fascinating website offers a glimpse into the world of opera, including detailed information on composers, libretti, and performance histories.

PUTTING IT ALL TOGETHER

1.   Study the life and works of Leonardo da Vinci. Be able to answer the following questions:

> What kind of education did da Vinci receive?
> What were some of his major discoveries?
> What were some of da Vinci's greatest artistic works?
> What scientific experiments did he conduct?

Someone who is well educated and has many different abilities and interests is known as a "Renaissance Man." In what ways was da Vinci a true "Renaissance Man"?

2.   What were the most significant works of Boccaccio and Dante? Research these two authors: what were their most famous works? What were the topics and dates of these works? Boccaccio's work was set during the time of what historical tragedy?

3.   Study the images of Brunelleschi's dome. Why was it so remarkable when it was built? Also, study images of St. Mark's Basilica in Venice. How are these two spaces alike? How are they different? Which one is older?

4.   Explore the history of Florence. Visit http://www.aboutflorence.com/history-of-Florence.html

5.   Spend some time visiting the Baroque instruments website: how do these instruments differ from their modern versions?

6.   The years from 1550 to 1700 spanned an incredible period of scientific development. Many modern discoveries were made, based upon the study of chemistry, zoology, botany, pharmacology, natural sciences, and the human body. Spend some time researching the lives and works of Newton and Leibniz. Who were their contemporaries? How were they educated? What were some of their most important discoveries?

VIEWING GUIDE

1.   We use the term _____ to describe the approximately three hundred years from 1600 to 1900 when music

_____

_____.

2.   There are six common qualities of music during the Common Practice Era, including (provide 3) _____

_____

_____.

3.   The city of _____ was a perfect city for artistic experimentation during the Renaissance. Famous residents included

_____.

4.   The most significant new genre of the Common Practice Era invented in Florence had various names at first, but eventually would be called _____.

5.   The term "Renaissance" means _____.

6.   Increased focus on human achievement is usually called

_____.

7.   The career of Italian composer _____ spanned the late Renaissance into the Baroque Era. His musical style changed from _____ to _____.

8.   The 1607 opera *Orfeo* was called a _____.

9.   Opera is essentially a _____ where all (or part) of the script is _____.

10.   *Instrumentation* means _____.

11.   What architectural structure inspired Gabrieli's compositions?

_____.

12.   In Greek mythology, who was Orpheus? _____

_____.

13. A _____ is a theatrical requirement for ending a Baroque drama.

14. Many of the stories upon which Baroque operas (even modern ones) are based can be traced back to _____.

15. "Baroque" is a French word for the Portuguese *barrôco* which meant _____. Initially the term (circle one) was / was not positive in meaning?

16. Monophony means _____. Writing down music by hand in what we call _____ was actually a high-tech skill. Throughout the Medieval period, music became more _____.

17. *Basso continuo* is created by how many players, playing what kinds of instruments? _____
_____.

18. Two popular Baroque genres of pieces for keyboard, lute, or guitar were the _____ (from the Italian verb "to touch") and the _____.

19. A fugue is a _____.

20. *Recitative* conveys primarily _____, while an *aria* is _____.

21. Serious Baroque opera based on mythology became known as _____. In the early 18th-century, short, comic episodes called _____ were placed between the acts of these serious works.

22. Throughout the Baroque era, who could afford to sponsor operatic productions? _____

23. The word _____ means "work" in Latin. Later the Italian form, _____, came to describe the whole genre of staged, sung works.

UNIT 6

LITURGICAL CALENDAR, STREET PARTIES, AND THE NEW CHURCH MUSIC

FIGURES

Georg Friedrich Handel
(1685-1759)

*George I of Hanover
(1660-1727)

PLACES

Bologna, Italy
Rio de Janeiro, Brazil
New Orleans, Louisiana

VOCABULARY

Liturgical (*leitos*=public) + (*ergos*=performing, doing)
The schedule of celebrations and ceremonies that mark the progression of the church year.   The "liturgical" calendar maintains a year-round schedule of the liturgies, or worship services that should be observed.

Advent
The four weeks of the liturgical calendar leading up to Christmas Eve.

Lent
The forty days of fasting and preparation prior to Easter (excluding Sundays, which are always Feast Days).

Weiberfasnacht
Also known as *giovedí grasso* in Italian.   The Thursday before Ash Wednesday. Women enjoy popular traditions for celebrating this night including, in some countries, cutting the necktie of any man found wearing one.

Rosenmontag

Also known as "Rose Monday" in English, this is the Monday before Ash Wednesday. Many cities stage lavish parades on this day, featuring floats bedecked with flowers.

Mardi Gras (*mardi*=Tuesday) + (*gras*=fat)

Also known as *Fasnacht* in German, and "Shrove" or "Fat Tuesday" in English, this is the Tuesday just before Ash Wednesday (the beginning of Lent). It is the last big celebration day of Carnival. Pancakes dripping in butter and syrup are traditionally associated with this day.

Carnival (*carne*=meat) + (*vale*=farewell). Also Carnaval and Carnevale.

Known as **Fasching** in German, Carnival is an unofficial period marking the celebrations that lead up to Ash Wednesday and the forty days of Lenten fasting before Easter. It is not part of the Liturgical Calendar, but has grown in popular practice.

Oratorio

From the Italian verb to speak or pray, *orare*. The oratorio is a musical setting of a text, primarily Biblical or sacred. Developed at the end of the Renaissance, early sacred oratorios would be performed in a section of the church adjacent to the sanctuary known as the *Oratorium*—a hall for prayer and preaching, something like today's Sunday School Room. The oratorio gained great popularity during the Baroque period as an entertainment appropriate to the Lenten season. Like an opera, the oratorio begins with text, or a libretto, that is set to music for soloists, chorus, and instrumental ensemble. Unlike opera, however, oratorio is not "staged" (no costumes, acting, or sets).

Passion

A subset of oratorio, a "passion" is an oratorio based specifically on the story of Christ's crucifixion and his suffering.

Cantata

From the Italian *cantare*, "to sing." This musical genre became very popular during the Baroque era as the principal form of sacred music. Composers such as J.S. Bach and Handel composed hundreds of cantatas for use in weekly church services. The cantata was integrated into the new Protestant (Lutheran) church services.

DATES

1710:	Handel leaves Germany for England.
1710-1727:	Reign of King George I, England
1715:	Louis XIV dies.

1718:	New Orleans founded.
1730:	Benjamin Franklin begins to publish *Poor Richard's Almanack*.
1733:	Georgia, the last of the thirteen American colonies, founded.
1739:	**Handel's oratorio *Saul* has its premiere.**
1742:	**Handel's oratorio *The Messiah* has its premiere in Dublin, Ireland.**

LISTENING

George Handel	Chorus: ***And He Shall Purify* from *The Messiah*, HWV 56 (1741)** (CD1/tr16) Chorus: *Hallelujah* Chorus*: Amen*
J.S. Bach	*Oratorium tempore navitatis Christi* (Christmas Oratorio), BWV 248 (1734) Chorus: Jauchzet frohlocket!

WEBSITES

http://www.naxos.com/person/George_Frideric_Handel/24403.htm
The official Naxos site on Handel, including biographical information and images.
For more information, see:
http://gfhandel.org/
http://www2.nau.edu/~tas3/handel.html

http://classical-music-opera.com/george-frederic-handel/history-timeline.html
More information on Handel's life.
http://gfhandel.org/messiah.htm
Visit this page for specific information on Handel's *Messiah*, including the history of the premier in 1742.

http://www.classicalnotes.net/classics/watermusic.html
Specific information on Handel's *Watermusic* and *Music for the Royal Fireworks.*

http://www.bach-cantatas.com/
A website devoted to the cantatas of J. S. Bach.

http://www.englishmonarchs.co.uk/hanover.htm
An introduction to the life and reign of Britain's King George I, who loved Handel's music but never learned to speak English!

http://www.wf-f.org/LiturgicalCalendar-info.html
Visit this website for information on the liturgical calendar and an explanation of the major feast days.

http://www.venetianmasksshop.com/history.htm
A brief history on the famous carnival celebration in Venice, Italy. This particular website sells authentic, custom-made masks fashioned by the celebrated Venetian *mascareri* (mask-makers). Select your favorite at:
http://www.venetianmasksshop.com/index.html

Parental Note: The material on the following pages is safe for all ages, but does include a number of links that may or may not be appropriate for some students. Remember that Carnival has always been (and continues to be) largely an adult celebration.

http://www.twistedimage.com/productions/carnivale/
More colorful sites describing the history and characters of Carnival. Also view:
http://www.ilcarnevale.it/storiamenu.htm
http://www.ilcarnevale.it/maschereinglese.htm
http://www.delpiano.com/carnival/html/venice_car.html

PUTTING IT ALL TOGETHER

1.   Visit the Carnival (Carnaval/Carnivale) websites, and read the descriptions of the characteristics and personalities of the following *commedia dell'arte* personalities:

- Harlequin
- Pantelone
- Capitano
- Brighella

- Columbina

Also: What kind of costume was worn by *El Medico dea Peaste*? Why? What was the practical purpose for wearing masks during Carnival (why was it helpful to be disguised)?

2.   Study the life of Handel. What kind of musical training did he receive? Did he come from a musical family? Look carefully at the genres of music that he composed: did he only compose music of one type, or was he equally capable of both sacred and secular music? How are his oratorios a good example of this?

3.   Spend some time getting acquainted with the liturgical calendar. Depending upon your denomination and/or religion, you will probably see many feasts and celebrations that are familiar to you—maybe you know them all! Calculate which liturgical season is current while studying this unit. What do you know about it? What influence does the liturgical calendar have on the colors used inside the church (on the altar, or on the stole the pastor/priest will wear)?

4.   Do people in your community celebrate Mardi Gras/Carnival? If so, how? Who organizes the festivities? Is it a draw for tourism? If not, why not? Try to determine the nearest place to your home where Carnival is celebrated.

VIEWING GUIDES

1.   A text is considered _____ if the story deals with a religious theme, and _____ if it is concerned primarily with worldly (non-church) topics. Purely instrumental music (without text) can be considered "sacred" if _____

_____.

2.   Martin Luther allegedly uttered, "Why should the Devil get all of the good tunes?" because _____

_____.

3.   In a Christian context, a liturgy is a general term for _____. In Eastern Christianity (Orthodoxy), a liturgy always means a service that celebrates

_____.

4.   A liturgical calendar lays out _____.
Some celebrations have fixed dates, like _____,
and others are linked to the lunar calendar, like _____

_____ .

5.   Theaters were traditionally closed in the summertime because
_____ , but they
were closed during Lent because _____

_____ .

6.   When faced with the prospect of a long period of fasting, people
tended to _____ .
That made the pre-Lenten season an obvious season for performances
of _____ . Why? _____ .
In addition, people attended _____ .

7.   In the United States, Carnival, or *Mardi Gras,* is celebrated with
great gusto in _____ (city) because _____

_____

_____ .

8.   For each Carnival season, composers prepared _____ .
For   the   Lenten   season,   the   same   composers   would   write
_____ . Why? _____ .

9.   An oratorio was not performed inside of the _____ .
A cantata could be sacred or secular, and the sacred ones were indeed
performed (where?) _____ .

10.   Oratorios were initially in _____ parts, and in the middle was a
_____ .

11.   Stories from the (circle one) Old Testament / New Testament
make the best oratorio topics because _____

_____ .

12.   Oratorios that tell the story of Christ's crucifixion are called
_____ .

UNIT 7

A LIVELY JOURNEY THROUGH THE LIFE OF JOHANN SEBASTIAN BACH

FIGURES

Johann Sebastian Bach
(1685-1750)

Georg Philipp Telemann
(1681-1767)

Antonio Vivaldi
(1678-1741)

Georg Friedrich Handel
(1685-1759)

Dietrich Buxtehude
(1637-1707)

Marin Mersenne
(1588-1648)

Sir Isaac Newton
(1642-1727)

Jean D'Alembert
(1717-1783)

Denis Diderot
(1713-1784)

Johann Gottfried Walther
(1684-1748)

Johann Gottfried Herder
(1744-1803)

Carl Philipp Emanuel Bach
(1714-1788)

Johann Christian Bach
(1735-1782)

Frederick II ("the Great") of Prussia
(1712-1786)

*Johann Quantz
(1697-1773)

PLACES
All places are in modern-day Germany

Eisenach
Ohrdruf
Lüneberg
Arnstadt
Lübeck
Mühlhausen
Weimar
Cöthen (Köthen)
Leipzig
Berlin

VOCABULARY

Doctrine of Affections
Known in German as *Affektenlehre* (*Affekt*=affect or emotion) + (*Lehre*=teaching), the Doctrine of Affections was an important foundation of Baroque aesthetics, especially as applied to arts. According to the theory, an art like music was capable of "affecting" the hearer in powerful ways. Because of this power, it was believed, music should express one consistent affect (or emotion) throughout each given section or movement rather than shifting from one affect to another.

Pastorale
From the Latin *pastor*, or shepherd. Music reflecting a "pastoral affect" had a calm and peaceful sound, reminding listeners of shepherds in green pastures, herding sheep (a favorite theme of painters in the Baroque period). Any movement entitled *Pastorale* was intended to evoke images of flocks grazing under the protective eye of a shepherd in a beautiful natural setting.

Siciliano
Another common style or "affect" of Baroque music, movements marked *Siciliano* were also "pastoral," but often in a minor key.

Collegia Musica
Informal groups of "musical colleagues" who would meet to discuss and play music together. These groups promoted what ultimately would become public concerts.

Sanssouci
From the French *sans souci* (*sans*=without) + (*souci*=troubles), this was the name of Frederick the Great's palace in Potsdam outside of Berlin, sometimes called his "Pleasure Palace." Sanssouci was designed as a royal get-away and a small version of Versailles, the famous French palace. Frederick himself designed many aspects of his palace and the surrounding park.

DATES

1640-1659:	English Civil War
1660:	English Monarchy Restored.
1678:	**Antonio Vivaldi is born.**
1681:	Pennsylvania founded by William Penn.
1682:	Rene-Robert La Salle explores the lower Mississippi Valley region, claims it for France, and names it "Louisiana."
1685:	**J.S. Bach is born.**
1750:	**Death of J.S. Bach**
1754-1763:	The French and Indian War (fought in America)
1756-1763:	Seven Years' War (fought in Europe)
1790:	Benjamin Franklin dies

LISTENING

J.S. Bach	**French Suite No. 5 in G Major, "Gavotte" BWV 816 (1722)** (CD1/tr12)
	***Jesu, bleibet meine Freude*, Cantata 147 (1723)** (CD1/tr13)

Recitative: *Du böses Kind* (CD1/tr14) and **Aria:** *Ei! Wie schmeckt der Kaffee süsse* **(1734)** (CD1/tr15) from the *Coffee Cantata*, BWV 211

Toccata and Fugue in D minor, BWV 565 (1708) (CD1/tr8)

Brandenburg Concerto No. 2 in F major, BWV 1047: Allegro, Andante, Allegro assai (1717) (CD1/tr9-11)

Brandenburg Concerto No. 5 in D major, BWV 1050 (1720)

Prelude and Fugue: Begin with No 1 in C major, BWV 846 (From the *Well-Tempered Clavier,* Book I, 1722)

Italian Concerto, BWV 971 (1735)

Antonio Vivaldi   *The Four Seasons* (*Il quattro stagioni*) (1723)
Concerto No. 1 in E major ("Spring"), RV 269
Concerto No. 2 in G minor ("Summer"), RV 315
Concerto No. 3 in F major ("Autumn"), RV 293
Concerto No. 4 in F minor ("Winter"), RV 297

George Handel   **Concerto Grosso No. 6 in D Major, HWV 317 (op. 3)** (CD1/tr17)

WEBSITES

http://www.naxos.com/person/Georg_Philipp_Telemann/23879.htm
The official Naxos site on Telemann, including biographical information, images, listening lists, and audio files. Also see:
http://www.baroquemusic.org/bqxtel.html
http://www.uni-magdeburg.de/magdeburg/telemann_eng.html

http://www.fuguemasters.com/telemann.html
This site outlines some interesting parallels, and differences, between Telemann and Sebastian Bach, and also explains why Telemann is in the Guinness Book of World Records!

http://www.naxos.com/composerinfo/Antonio_Vivaldi/22387. htm
The official Naxos site on Vivaldi, including biographical information, images, listening lists, and audio files. Also see:
http://www.baroquemusic.org/bqxvivaldi.html

http://www.baroquecds.com/vivaldiseasons.html
A guide to Vivaldi's famous "Four Seasons" violin concerti, including the descriptive titles Vivaldi gave to the movements and the sonnets (written by Vivaldi himself) that go with each movement.

http://www.naxos.com/person/George_Frideric_Handel/24403.ht m
The official Naxos site on Handel, including biographical information, images, listening lists, and audio files. Also see:
http://gfhandel.org/
http://www2.nau.edu/~tas3/handel.html

http://www.naxos.com/person/Dieterich_Buxtehude/27114.htm
The official Naxos site on Buxtehude, including biographical information, listening lists, and audio files. Also see:
http://www.classical.net/music/comp.lst/buxtehude.php
http://www.dieterich-buxtehude.org/english/english.html

http://www.nndb.com/people/576/000107255/
Although his name is not as well-known as that of his friend Descartes, visit this site to discover what important contributions Mersenne made to modern philosophy and music theory.

http://www.newton.ac.uk/newtlife.html
Information on the life and discoveries of Sir Isaac Newton.

http://www.gap-system.org/~history/Mathematicians/D'Alembert.html
Information on the life and works of Jean D'Alembert.

http://www.iep.utm.edu/d/diderot.htm
An introduction to the life and works of Diderot. Also visit:
http://www.kirjasto.sci.fi/diderot.htm
http://history-world.org/diderot.htm

http://plato.stanford.edu/entries/herder/
http://www.iep.utm.edu/g/germidea.htm
These two sites offer an introduction to the life and works of Herder, as well as an overview of the German Idealism movement, of which Herder was an important part.

http://www.naxos.com/person/Carl_Philipp_Emanuel_Bach/17646.htm
The official Naxos site on C.P.E. Bach, including biographical information, images, listening lists, and audio files. Also visit:
http://www2.nau.edu/~tas3/cpebach.html

http://www.naxos.com/person/Johann_Christian_Bach/17647.htm
The official Naxos site on J.C. Bach, including biographical information, images, listening lists, and audio files. Also visit:
http://www.classical.net/music/comp.lst/bachjc.php

http://www.hoasm.org/XIB/XIBCourtFrederickGreat.html
An introduction to the life and times of Frederick II of Prussia, commonly known as "The Great." Find out some of the things that made him one of the most powerful men of his time, as well as one of Europe's most influential monarchs. Also visit:
http://german-history.suite101.com/article.cfm/frederick_the_great
http://www.spsg.de/index.php/id=163

http://www.flutehistory.com/Players/Johann_Joachim_Quantz/index.php3
An introduction to the life and works of Quantz and his position in the court of Frederick the Great. Read about his important role in woodwind (specifically flute) pedagogy.

PUTTING IT ALL TOGETHER

1.   Using the map of your choice and the list of "PLACES," trace the routes that Sebastian Bach would have traveled between his stations. Begin by marking each station, and labeling the years that Bach would have spent there, then draw a line directly from the first station to the next. You may even want to discover the modern-day population of each of these cities. Below is the list of cities and years:

- Eisenach: 1685-1695

- Ohrdruf: 1695-1700
- Lüneberg: 1700-1702
- Arnstadt: 1703-1707
- Mühlhausen: 1707-1708
- Weimar: 1708-1717
- Cöthen (Köthen): 1717-1722
- Leipzig: 1723-1750

2.   Antonio Vivaldi was a very popular Baroque composer with a high-profile career. Carefully examine the websites on Vivaldi and answer the following questions for both Vivaldi and Bach.

- What was each composer's chief instrument?
- In addition to composing, what musical job did each hold?
- Though each composer was a teacher, which gender of students did each specifically teach?
- By which church (Protestant/Catholic) was each employed?
- What were the cities like where each man spent significant numbers of years? (You may need to do a little research on Venice in order to answer this question!)
- For what kinds of ensembles did each composer write?
- What kind of ensemble did each composer seem to prefer? Why do you think so?
- Did either composer compose operas? Are they well-known?
- Finally, how prominent, or famous, was either composer during his lifetime?

3.   If you have not already done so, visit this website:

http://www.baroquecds.com/vivaldiseasons.html

Although parts of Vivaldi's first concerto are heard on recordings in many places, like in restaurants and television commercials, all four of these concerti are even more fabulous works to hear performed in an actual concert!

Take time to read each one of the sonnets that Vivaldi wrote to accompany his four concerti. Then listen to that concerto. Try to imagine it in live performance. You can even find some very beautiful video performances of *The Seasons* (www.netflix.com or www.amazon.com). Think about how the titles of the movements, and the music itself, will depict the images in the sonnets.

4.   By now you already know some things about Sebastian Bach's biography. Study the biographical information on Buxtehude; you may even wish to join the International Buxtehude Society! What relationship did Buxtehude have to Bach, and why did Bach turn down Buxtehude's job? The answer may surprise you!

5.   Research the lives of Bach's two most famous sons, C.P.E. and J.C. Bach:

- For what careers did each *begin* his advanced education and training?
- Which brother was older? How old was each when Sebastian Bach died?
- Which brother converted to Catholicism?
- In what genres of composition did each brother specialize? Remember: this is a direct reflection of the positions each held!
- Which brother wrote an important "treatise" on playing a particular instrument?
- Which brother had an influence on W.A. Mozart?
- Which was known as the "London" Bach?

6.   Place approximate dates for the following stylistic periods on a blank "Timeline." Remember that any kind of style gains and falls in popularity gradually — there is not an "official" date at which something becomes "in" or "out" of style:

- Rococo
- Stil galant
- Empfindsamer stil (Empfindsamkeit)

Use the following websites for help. Look carefully at the available images; what differences and similarities do you notice?

Rococo:
http://www.artlex.com/ArtLex/r/rococo.html
http://www.nvcc.edu/home/jwulff/MUS103/rococo_period.htm

Galant:
http://www.answers.com/topic/gallant

Empfindsamer stil:
http://www.answers.com/topic/empfindsamkeit
http://www.lcsproductions.net/MusHistRev/Terms/EmpfindsamerStil.html

VIEWING GUIDE

1.   It is useful to call Bach by his _____ name, _____, since so many males in his family had the same _____ name of _____.

2.   The _____ of the _____ was a very broad idea used to organize Baroque expression and aesthetics. In

short, something that started joyfully should _____
and *not* _____.

3.   We speak of Bach's various towns of residence/employment as
his _____.   He did move around a lot, but usually
because he _____.

4.   In his job in the town where his cousin Walther worked,
_____, he was primarily a _____, but he
got in trouble there because _____.

5.   In his next job at _____, he was writing a lot of court
music, which pleased him, but that job came to an end when

_____.

6.   Bach's longest-lasting job was in _____ and his
duties there included teaching and conducting the _____ at a
church called _____.   He also got very
involved in music performed at the trendy _____.
Those early groups of people who met to play music in public places
were laying the foundation for what we will later call the

_____.

7.   The most technologically advanced instrument of the era (indeed
one of the most technologically advanced *objects* of any kind) was the
_____.   It was powered by _____
who pumped the _____ to drive _____ through the
_____.   Today that function is accomplished by

_____.

8.   The _____ was a small basic keyboard instrument
that many people could afford.   It (circle one) was / was not appropriate
for public performance because _____.
Its appeal lay in the fact that, at an individual key level, the player could

_____.

9.   Bach's most successful son _____ worked for the
German   King   _____   at   the   court   in   (city)
_____.   This king loved the new keyboard instrument
_____.   He was also a marvelous flute player.

UNIT 8

ENLIGHTENMENT, CLASSICISM, AND
THE ASTONISHING MOZART

FIGURES

Antoine Watteau
(1684-1721)

Voltaire (François-Marie Arouet)
(1694-1778)

Denis Diderot
(1713-1784)

Jean-Jacques Rousseau
(1712-1778)

Thomas Jefferson
(1743-1826)

Leopold Mozart
(1719-1787)

Wolfgang Amadeus Mozart
(1756-1791)

Ludwig Köchel
(1800-1877)

Anton Stadler
(1753-1812)

Pierre Beaumarchais
(1732-1799)

Lorenzo da Ponte
(1749-1838)

Franz Joseph Haydn
(1732-1809)

Emperor Joseph II
(1741-1790)

*Empress Maria Theresa
(1717-1780)

Louis XVI
(1754-1793)

PLACES

Prague, Czech Republic
Bologna, Italy
Vienna, Austria
London, England
Paris, France
Ottoman Empire

VOCABULARY

Classical
From the Latin noun *classicus*, meaning first or upper class. A term used to describe European art and architecture starting in the second half of the 18th century. The artistic principles date back to classical antiquity. By extension, the term is applied loosely to music in the late eighteenth century.

Fortepiano
From the Italian words *forte* (strong, or loud) and *piano* (usually rendered "soft"—although another meaning is "smooth" or "graceful"). The instrument was also called a *pianoforte.* The word "forte" dropped away, leaving the name "piano." The *fortepiano* is the direct ancestor of the modern piano, and took its name from the fact that it was capable of playing both loudly and softly at the individual key level—something harpsichords, clavichords, and organs cannot do. The main feature of a *fortepiano* mechanism (action) is a hammer that strikes a string.

Rococo
From the French *rocaille*, meaning "debris" or "rubble." This style of fanciful early 18th-century art, architecture, and music reflected irregular but proportional natural shapes. Shells, pebbles, and vines are common decorative images in Rococo style.

Stil galant (*stil*=style)

From the French *galer*, meaning "to make merry" or "to make a show." This style of mid 18th-century art and architecture is reflected in paintings of what has been coined in this course as "clean sheep parties" or *fêtes galantes*, in which nobility would enjoy an idealized and cleaned-up version of "ordinary" natural life, accompanied by refreshments and dancing.

Empfindsamkeit (*Empfind*=sensitive) + (*sam*=ly) + (*keit*=ness)

This German word for "sensitivity" lends its name to *Empfindsamer Stil*, a style of music that was characteristic of the transition from Baroque to Romanticism. Music of this "style" featured sudden shifts from one "affect" (or emotion) to the next, evoking the sort of sudden changes one would find in the natural world (such as in weather, or in human nature!).

Sturm und Drang

From a literary movement that originated in Germany during the 1760s. Any art described as *Sturm und Drang* puts emphasis on psychological aspects, emotional affects, and the complexity of human nature.

Encyclopédists

This group of French scholars revived and further developed the ancient Greek fascination with collecting and organizing information. Its members included Diderot, Voltaire, and D'Alembert, as well as several others. They reflected a common Enlightenment ideal that education and knowledge would, in and of themselves, solve humanity's problems.

Divertimento

A composition for instrumental ensemble with several short movements, designed to be a light "diversion."

Köchel number

Mozart died before he could properly organize his compositions, plus many of his compositions had never been published. So any *opus* numbers attached to his pieces weren't sufficient. For that reason, a 19th-century German scholar named Ludwig Köchel undertook the huge task of putting Mozart's works into order and assigned them a "K." number. This kind of posthumous organization is necessary for many composers, and that's why, when you look at a concert program, or the contents of a recording, you find a variety of initials and complex letter/number designations after many composers' works.

Opera buffa

A type of opera that became very popular starting in the mid 18th century. *Opera buffa* had pleasant and funny plots, with lighter and more appealing styles of arias, in contrast to the serious plots and virtuosic arias of *opera seria*.

Drama giocoso

Mozart's own fusion of *opera seria* and *buffa*, this term was used for his opera *Don Giovanni*, which had several "layers" of story and meaning happening at one time. Although the layers all relate to one another and often feature the same characters, some layers are serious (deadly, even) while others are silly and romantic.

DATES

1754:	The Oriental Academy opens in Vienna, Austria.
1761:	**Haydn begins his employment for Prince Paul Anton Esterhàzy.**
1783:	The American Revolution ends.
1786:	***Marriage of Figaro* has its premiere in Vienna.**
1787:	***Don Giovanni* has its premiere in Prague.**
1789:	The French Revolution
1793:	King Louis XVI and Queen Marie Antoinette executed.
1794:	Eli Whitney receives a patent for the cotton gin.
1798:	**The premiere of Haydn's *The Creation***
1800:	Seat of American government moves from Philadelphia to Washington, D.C. The Library of Congress founded.

LISTENING

C.P.E. Bach	***L'Philippine*, Wq. 117/34, H. 96** (CD1/tr18)
Jean-Phillipe Rameau	Overture and Prologues from Scenes 1 and 2, *Les Indes gallants* (1735)
Joseph Haydn	***Allegro*. Trumpet Concerto in E-Flat major, HOB VIIe:1 (1796)** (CD1/tr19)
	The Creation (1798)

Symphony in F minor, H.I No. 49 (1768)

Symphony No. 94 in G Major ("Surprise"), H 1/94
(1791)

Wolfgang Mozart   *Allegro Molto,* **Symphony No. 40 in G minor, K. 550
(1788)** (CD1/tr20)

Concerto for Clarinet in A major, K. 622 (1791)

Rondo alla turca, **Piano Sonata No. 11 in A Major, K.
331(c. 1783)** (CD1/tr21)

"Lacrimosa," Requiem in D minor, K. 626 (1791)
Overture, *The Marriage of Figaro* (*Le nozze di Figaro*),
K. 497 (1786)

Violin Concerto No. 5 in A major, K. 219 (1775)
Andante, Piano Concerto No. 21 in C major, K. 467
(1785)

Don Giovanni. **Overture** (CD2/tr1); **Recitative:** *Alfin
siam* **liberati** (CD2/tr2); **Duet:** *La ci darem la mano*
(1787) (CD2/tr3)

WEBSITES

http://www.ibiblio.org/wm/paint/auth/watteau/
An introduction to the life and work of Watteau. Also view:
http://www.met.org/toah/hd/watt/hd_watt.htm
http://www.abcgallery.com/W/watteau/watteau.html

http://www.kirjasto.sci.fi/voltaire.htm
An introduction to the life and works of Voltaire. Also visit:
http://www.lucidcafe.com/library/95nov/voltaire.html
**http://www.wsu.edu:8080/~wldciv/world_civ_reader/world_civ_r
eader_2/voltaire.html**

http://www.iep.utm.edu/d/diderot.htm
An introduction to the life and work of Diderot, whose most significant work was his
Encyclopédie.
http://www.kirjasto.sci.fi/diderot.htm

http://history-world.org/diderot.htm

http://www.iep.utm.edu/e/encyclop.htm
An introduction to the *Encyclopedists*, and their adaptation of the ancient Greeks'
passion for cataloguing to the modern scientific approach.
http://www.sullivan-county.com/news/mine/servetus.htm
Older students will wish to read the following article, reprinted from 1868:
http://www.theatlantic.com/doc/186802/encyclopedists

http://www.lucidcafe.com/library/96jun/rousseau.html
An introduction to the life and works of Rousseau. Also visit:
http://www.iep.utm.edu/r/rousseau.htm

http://www.whitehouse.gov/about/presidents/thomasjefferson/
An introduction to Thomas Jefferson, one of America's greatest Presidents and
Founding Fathers as well as a great contributor to Enlightenment thinking in the
New World. Also visit:
http://www.monticello.org/
http://etext.virginia.edu/jefferson/
http://sc94.ameslab.gov/TOUR/tjefferson.html

http://www.mozartproject.org/biography/mozart_l.html
Information on the life and works of Mozart's father, Leopold Mozart. Also visit:
**http://www.naxos.com/composerinfo/Leopold_Mozart/21865.
htm**
http://www.hoasm.org/XIIC/MozartL.html
**http://classicalmusic.suite101.com/article.cfm/leopold_mozart_w
olfgangs_father**

**http://www.naxos.com/composerinfo/Wolfgang_Amadeus_Mozart
/15934.htm**
The official Naxos site on Mozart, including biographical information, images,
listening lists, and audio links. Also visit:
http://www.mozartproject.org/
http://www.mozarteum.at/

**http://americanhistory.suite101.com/article.cfm/italians_in_Amer
ica_lorenzo_da_ponte**
Study the fascinating life of Lorenzo da Ponte, who was at various times in his life a
scholar, priest, librettist, translator, and, after immigrating to America, a college
professor at Columbia.

http://lpil.info/index.php?option=com_content&task=view&id=16&Itemid=30

http://www.columbia.edu/cu/alumni/Magazine/Legacies/Beeson/Beeson.html

http://www.naxos.com/composerinfo/Franz_Joseph_Haydn/24410.htm

The official Naxos site on Haydn, including biographical information, images, listening links, and audio files. Also visit:

http://www.karadar.com/index.php/en/composers-biographies/article/1-composers-biographies/14654-haydn-franz-joseph.html

http://www.nndb.com/people/636/000101333/

A brief biography of Austrian Emperor Joseph II. Also visit:

http://www.newadvent.org/cathen/08508b.htm

http://www.aeiou.at/aeiou.encyclop.m/m208917.htm;internal&action=_setlanguage.action?LANGUAGE=en

An introduction to Empress Maria Theresa, mother to many kings and queens as well as one of Europe's most powerful monarchs. Also visit:

http://www.newadvent.org/cathen/09662d.htm

http://countrystudies.us/austria/17.htm

PUTTING IT ALL TOGETHER

1.   If you haven't done so already, visit the following site:

> http://www.wsu.edu:8080/~wldciv/world_civ_reader/world_civ_reader_2/voltaire.html

This is a brief (believe it or not!) excerpt of Voltaire's *Treatise on Toleration* (1863). Voltaire was considered one of the great "humanist" thinkers of the Enlightenment; although it is easy to see today how Humanism (and the focus on human beings) can be carried too far, take some time to think about how important these early Enlightenment ideas were. Do you agree with them? How are those ideas in evidence today? How are they abused today? Read this excerpt slowly: it is intended to be read one sentence at a time, and contemplated. Of course, it would be wonderful to contemplate while sitting in the gardens at Versailles . . . but that is something you'll have to arrange on your own! ☺

2.   Who were the "Encyclopedists"? Study the lives of Voltaire, Diderot, and Rousseau. What beliefs did they contribute to the "Enlightenment"? How did these beliefs contribute to the French and American Revolutions? In what different ways did Enlightenment thinkers define "nature," and where did human beings fit into nature?

3.   Study the life of Thomas Jefferson. What were some of his greatest achievements? For which three achievements did he, personally, wish to be remembered? (Visit the last-listed website to answer this question.) To what important American documents did he contribute? What can you currently see if you pay a visit to Monticello? What instrument did he play? Which parts of Europe did Jefferson visit?

4.   Although best known to history as "Wolfgang's father," Leopold Mozart was a successful and well-respected musician during his lifetime (perhaps even more "respectable" than his son!). What instrument was at the center of Leopold's life, and how did this influence the types of works he composed? What important book on playing an instrument did he write? What important contributions did he make to the lives of his children?

5.   Read about the life of Mozart's favorite (and eclectic!) librettist Lorenzo da Ponte. Where did he get his name (he was not born "Lorenzo da Ponte"), and which countries did he call home? How did he link up with Mozart? When did he move to the United States? What important work did he do in the U.S.?

6.   Compare and contrast the lives of Mozart and Haydn. For each composer, answer the following questions:

   - What kind of early education did he receive?
   - What kind of early musical training did he receive?
   - Did he come from a musical family?
   - Each had an "early" musical career, at a young age. How were those careers different?
   - Which composer did the most traveling?
   - Which composer had the steadiest employment?
   - Which composer wrote the most operas? The most symphonies?
   - Which composer wrote the most string quartets?
   - How many children did each composer have?

7.   How were Joseph II and Maria Theresa related? Through whom were both related to Louis XVI of France?

VIEWING GUIDE

1.   The unit begins with a comparison of the end of the Baroque era to the end of the Big Band Era after World War II. Points of similarity include _____

_____

_____.

2.   The term _____ is problematic, because it has meanings far beyond a specific period of music during Mozart's lifetime.

3.   A technique where the notes of a simple harmony are "activated" and played over and over, quickly, to energize the harmony is called

_____.

4.   The eighteenth century is an era of Absolute _____, including Frederick the Great of _____, Catherine the Great of _____, and Joseph II of _____.

5.   There was a royal passion for collecting _____

_____.

6.   The term _____ came from a word meaning "rock debris" and featured natural designs like shells, leaves, and vines.

7.   Art or music described as *stil* _____ is characterized by _____. The painter _____ was so popular, even a new style of "natural" or informally draped clothing was named for him.

8.   _____ is primarily a German 18th-century literary movement that stressed dark and emotional ideas, but the term was applied also to some music.

9.   Another German term, *Empfindsamkeit*, means _____ style. It stood in direct contrast to the old aesthetic—the Doctrine of the _____ —where all emotions were constant in an individual movement or section of music.

10.   Bach's _____ were far more modern than he, and they embraced new ideas. One worked in Berlin for the _____ King named _____.

11.   The _____ is a *very* soft instrument, and very sensitive, but too soft to be suitable for public performance.

12.   Three interesting features of a piano action, as demonstrated by Michael Inman at Steinway Hall: _____

_____

_____

_____.

13.   The _____ was associated with aristocracy in Europe, but the new keyboard instrument, the _____, was not. An _____ has the same mechanism, but it's turned at a 90-degree angle to fit in a smaller space.

14.   The most famous Enlightenment figure in America was _____.

15.   The Eastern-European city that embraced Mozart's music strongly: _____.

16.   Mozart was Austrian-born, but his music was so often written in _____ style. This style dominated European music in the 18th century.   Only the country of _____ consistently resisted this style in favor of its own.

17.   Mozart was fond of a newly invented (18th century) wind instrument called the _____ and he wrote music for a well-known virtuoso who made his career on this instrument.

18.   Europeans in the 18th century found anything _____ fashionable and exotic.

19.   *Opera* _____ became more popular than *opera* _____ in Mozart's day. Spoken-dialogue operas called _____ were also popular. Mozart's _____ is a famous example.

20.   Both Mozart and his librettist _____ chose to set to music a French play that had been banned. The resulting opera was called _____.

21.   Haydn had a different mentality than Mozart.   For example,

_____

_____.

22.   Haydn was a genius at writing _____ and wrote more than one hundred. He also wrote a great deal of music for the _____, a strange stringed instrument favored by his patron the Count.

23.   Haydn was very clever in how he set the words in his oratorio *The Creation,* especially the section _____.

UNIT 9

INTO THE ABYSS: THE STRUGGLE WITH UNFETTERED IMAGINATION

FIGURES

Napoleon Bonaparte
(1769-1821)

Josephine Beauharnais Bonaparte
(1763-1814)

Jacques-Louis David
(1748-1825)

Carl Spitzweg
(1808-1885)

Wilhelm Wackenroder
(1773-1798)

Ludwig Tieck
(1773-1853)

Boethius
(c. 480-c. 525)

Samuel Coleridge
(1772-1834)

E.T.A. Hoffmann
(1776-1822)

Sir Walter Scott
(1771-1832)

Lord George Gordon Byron
(1788-1824)

Jakob (1785-1863) **and Wilhelm** (1786-1859) **Grimm**

Mary Shelley
(1797-1851)

Edgar Allan Poe
(1809-1849)

Francisco de Goya
(1746-1828)

Johann von Goethe
(1749-1832)

Friedrich Schiller
(1759-1805)

Caspar David Friedrich
(1774-1840)

PLACES

Corsica, France
Moscow, Russia
Elba, Italy
Paris, France

VOCABULARY

Romance
A literary style that focuses on imagination and human emotion. This term refers both to an era in European cultural history (the 19th century) and to an aesthetic approach that leaves behind the logic and rationalism found in the Enlightenment.

Gemütlichkeit
Defined as "good nature, sociability, coziness," this unique German term refers to the homey, "good-feeling-ness" that characterized the early Romantic period, especially as people recovered from the trauma of the Napoleonic Wars.

Novel
A literary genre that became popular during the 18th century and flourished during the Romantic era. Novels are fictional works that tell a story. They can be written in *narrative* form with *dramatic* (interactive) characters. Novels can also be written as an exchange of letters, called an *epistolary* novel. A short novel is called a *novella*.

Musica instrumentalis, musica humana, and musica mundana
Boethius' three divisions of music, from the physical to the divine: *Musica instrumentalis* is music of physical objects (instruments), *musica humana* is the music made by air passing through humans (singing), and *musica mundana* is the music of the spheres.

DATES

1788:	U.S. Constitution ratified
1789:	French Revolution
1789-1793:	Reign of Terror
1797:	John Adams elected second U.S. President
1804	Coronation of Napoleon
1804-1806:	Lewis and Clark Expedition
1805:	Battle of Austerlitz
1812:	Battle of Borodino
1814:	Napoleon exiled to Elba
1814-1815:	Congress of Vienna
1815:	Napoleon defeated in Battle of Waterloo
1818:	*Frankenstein: A Modern Prometheus* by Mary Shelley
1819:	*Ivanhoe* by Sir Walter Scott
1834:	Slavery abolished in British Empire
1840-1860:	Oregon Trail established as main highway to the Northwestern U.S.
1859:	*A Tale of Two Cities* by Charles Dickens

LISTENING

Charles Joseph Rouget de Lisle	*Marseillaise* (1792)
Ludwig van Beethoven	Symphony No. 3 in E-Flat major ("Eroica"), Op. 55 (1803) *Allegro con Brio*
	Wellington's Victory ("The Battle Symphony"), Op. 91 (1813)
Franz Schubert	*Gretchen am Spinnrade* (*Gretchen at the Spinning Wheel*), Op. 2, D. 118 (1814)
Felix Mendelssohn	Symphony No. 3 in A minor ("Scottish"), Op. 56 (1842)
Franz Liszt	*Mephisto Waltz* No. 1 (1862)
	Faust Symphony, S. 108 (1857)
Peter Tchaikovsky	***1812 Overture*, Op. 49 (1880)** (CD3/tr6)
	Liturgy of St. John Chrysostom, Op. 41 (1878)
	Nutcracker Ballet, Op. 71 (1892)
Jacques Offenbach	*Tales of Hoffmann* (1881, posthumous premiere) (DVD)

WEBSITES

http://www.lucidcafe.com/library/95aug/napoleon.html
An introduction to the life and military conquests of Napoleon. Also view:
http://www.bbc.co.uk/history/historic_figures/bonaparte_napoleon.shtml
http://www.napoleonguide.com/leaders_napoleon.htm

http://www.history.com/topics/french-revolutionary-and-napoleonic-wars

http://www.napoleonguide.com/josephine.htm
Biographical information on Napoleon's first Empress, Josephine. Older students
will want to visit:

http://www.ibiblio.org/wm/paint/auth/david/
An introduction to the life and works of David, one of the most celebrated artists to
observe and record images of the French Revolution. Also view:
http://www.artchive.com/artchive/D/david.html
http://www.abcgallery.com/D/david/david.html

http://www.answers.com/topic/carl-spitzweg
A brief biography of Spitzweg. Click below to see his best-known work:
http://www.penwith.co.uk/artofeurope/spitzweg.htm

http://www.newadvent.org/cathen/02610b.htm
An introduction to the life and works of Boethius, an important early philosopher
and martyr. Also view:
http://plato.stanford.edu/entries/boethius/

http://www.online-literature.com/coleridge/
An introduction to Samuel Coleridge, the father of the English Romantic Movement.
Older students, or any fan of Coleridge's work, will also wish to view:
http://www.gutenberg.org/browse/authors/c#a95

http://www.litgothic.com/Authors/hoffmann.html
A brief introduction to the works of E.T.A. Hoffmann and his colorful 19th-century
life. Also view:
http://www.kirjasto.sci.fi/hoffman.htm
http://www.litencyc.com/php/speople.php?rec=true&UID=2162

http://www.online-literature.com/walter_scott/
An introduction to the works and colorful life of Sir Walter Scott. Also view:
http://www.lucidcafe.com/library/95aug/scott.html
http://www.kirjasto.sci.fi/wscott.htm

http://englishhistory.net/byron.html
An introduction to the life and works of Byron. Also view:
http://www.online-literature.com/byron/
http://www.internationalbyronsociety.org/index.php?option=com
_frontpage&Itemid=1
Older students may wish to visit:

http://www.neuroticpoets.com/byron/

http://www.kirjasto.sci.fi/wgrimm.htm
http://www.kirjasto.sci.fi/jgrimm.htm
Information on the "Brothers Grimm," whose collections of *Kinder- und Hausmärchen* (*Children's and Household Tales*) were a key publication in the Romantic era.

http://www.kirjasto.sci.fi/mshelley.htm
An introduction to the life and works of Mary Shelley, daughter of early feminist author Mary Wollstonecraft and wife of Percy Bysshe Shelley, a friend of Lord Byron. Also view:
http://www.online-literature.com/shelley_mary/
http://www.litgothic.com/Authors/mshelley.html

http://www.online-literature.com/poe/
Information on the life and works of Poe, one of the most important American authors of the 19th century and one of the first "American" Romantics. Also view:
http://www.poemuseum.org/
http://www.eapoe.org/
http://www.poestories.com/

http://www.metmuseum.org/toah/hd/goya/hd_goya.htm
An introduction to the life and many styles of works of the Spanish "Master of Macabre." Also view:
http://www.ibiblio.org/wm/paint/auth/goya/
NOTE: Parents should review the contents and contexts of these sites; Goya's images were intended as shocking social commentary, and may not be suitable for younger students.

http://www.kirjasto.sci.fi/goethe.htm
An introduction to the life and works of Goethe. You will encounter him in following units; start getting acquainted today!

http://www.kirjasto.sci.fi/schiller.htm
Biographical information on leading 18th-century author and poet Friedrich Schiller. Also view:
http://www.theatrehistory.com/german/schiller.html
http://www.studiocleo.com/librarie/schiller/schillerpage.html

http://www.artchive.com/artchive/F/friedrich.html
Enjoy the ethereal works of early German Romantic artist Caspar David Friedrich. Also view:
http://www.metmuseum.org/special/Caspar_David_Friedrich/mo onwatchers_images.htm
http://www.caspardavidfriedrich.org/

VIEWING GUIDE

1.   The first thing to realize about the Romantic era is how important _____ is (and always has been) to Europeans.

2.   Romanticism developed in stages. First, in the early part of the 19th century, artists became fascinated by _____ _____.
They also looked into their national _____ and collected their national _____. Using all this material, in a kind of Stage Three, they set about creating _____ _____.

3.   The term *Romantic* or *Romanticism* means many things, including _____ _____.

4.   The English writer _____, in his novel _____, gave one of the best literary portraits of the French Revolutionary period and the many difficult situations that followed.   That novel opens with a famous line: _____.

5.   Napoleon may have come out of the intellectual era focused on rationalism, known as _____, but it was the old-fashioned issue of conquering and grabbing power that led him to be _____ at _____ Cathedral in 1804.

6.   The painter _____ showed Napoleon in all his glory. But his glory turned to ashes when he tried, ill-advisedly, to

conquer _____ in _____. The Russians survived, and then triumphed, by _____.
The parallels in this campaign with a campaign waged by _____
_____ in the 20th century are chilling.

7.   After the Napoleonic Wars, people drew inward, seeking stability and comfort. A style of furnishing and art called _____ was launched. A fine German painter named _____ captured the mood well. There is even a German term for "comfortable" that is used to describe this era: _____. Meanwhile, a long series of peace conferences called the _____ tried to put the Old Europe back together.

8.   We can use the words from an 18th-century German novel called *Joseph Berlinger* to see how the new Romantic authors _____ _____. Artists were definitely leaving behind a Classical view of music. In fact, suddenly the arts became _____.

9.   It's interesting to see the old three-part Greek view of music, starting at the top with _____ (music of the _____), followed by _____ (music made by human beings), and finally _____ (music made by physical objects like instruments).

10.   The Berlin writer _____ idolized the composer _____. In his writings, he talks about music in very emotional language with words like _____. His stories are often about musicians, but his most famous story is known to us as _____.

11.   Another writer who packed a power-punch was the English novelist _____. His novels were huge hits. Then there was the Romantic English poet _____. He died quite young. He, like the composer _____ was fascinated by the story of Don Juan, or, in Italian, Don Giovanni.

12.   The German writers known as _____ collected and published volumes of important fairy tales. Fairy tales

really aren't for children, because _____
_____.

13.   Maybe the most famous novel about the "supernatural" in the 19th century was Mary Shelley's _____ in 1818. And the most famous American poem about a spooky threatening bird, _____, was written by our great Romantic writer _____.

14.   The Romantic era was also a time when people began to research and understand the problem of _____ better. Sir Walter Scott incorporated this theme in his novels, including one that became the plot for a famous opera _____.

15.   But the most significant of all the Romantic writers was a German author named _____. He became famous in his twenties when he wrote a short novel called _____. _____. It was essentially the story of a love triangle, carried forth as a novel in "letter" form, which we call an _____. But this one was strange because the letters went only _____. The story ends with the _____ of the main character _____.

16.   Goethe got invited to live in _____, and he went, living quite (circle one) poorly / well for the rest of his life. There he wrote (for years) the most significant work of his career, the play _____. The entire Part I of this work turns on a _____ that the Professor makes with the _____. At issue is whether or not the _____ can grant the Professor one _____. If so, the _____ wins his _____.

17.   Another great German poet and playwright living in the same city towards the end of his life was _____.

A COMPARISON OF ENLIGHTMENT TO ROMANTICISM

"O, then I close my eyes to all the strife of the world—and withdraw quietly into the land of music, as into the land of belief."

Joseph Berlinger by William
Wackenroder (1773-1798)

Eighteenth Century Enlightenment	Nineteenth Century Romanticism
Music is an expression of balance and reason.	Music expresses the three "E's": emotion, enthusiasm, ecstasy.
Music is a rational and highly structured art.	Music is a spiritual, sublime, and inexplicable experience.
Music is a *social* experience.	Music is an individual revelation.
Music teaches us about this world.	Music teaches us about "other" worlds.
Music and musicians may appear as ordinary features and characters within a novel.	Musicians appear as fantastic literary characters, tossed about by unpredictable power of creativity.
Instruments are seen as physically beautiful: harpsichords are inlaid with mother-of-pearl; the insides of the lids are beautifully decorated; a gold flute is a status symbol.	Physical instruments represent the wretched limitations of music making: mere wood, strings, and wire – necessary, but not satisfactory for the sublime music composers want to write.
High melodies are emphasized, especially soprano and castrati.	Alto, baritone, and bass registers are "discovered" and exploited by composers.
Instruments that play in high registers are celebrated – flutes, oboe, trumpets, violins, plus the crispness and brilliance of the harpsichord.	Sustaining or "endless" instruments (not limited by breath) are preferred: piano, horns and low brass, viola, cello, bass, English horn, bassoon.

UNIT 10

BEETHOVEN AS HERO AND REVOLUTIONARY

FIGURES

Ludwig van Beethoven
(1770-1827)

Napoleon Bonaparte
(1769-1821)

Caspar David Friedrich
(1774-1840)

William Herschel
(1738-1822)

Carl Zelter
(1758-1832)

Johann Wolfgang von Goethe
(1749-1832)

PLACES

Bonn, Germany
Cologne, Germany
Vienna, Austria
Heiligenstadt, Austria
Weimar, Germany

VOCABULARY

Revolutionary
This adjective can be applied to anything that is related to, inspired by, or that brings about, revolution.   Usually, revolution indicates the overthrowing of something, whether it is a government, or a long-held theory. For example, many

nations have fought a "Revolutionary War," and many important scientific discoveries are the result of a "revolutionary" new idea.

Sturm und Drang (*sturm*= storm) + (*und*= and) + (*Drang*: from *dringen*, to press, urge, come through)

The *Sturm und Drang* aesthetic movement drew its name from the title of a novel, written in 1776 by German novelist Friedrich von Klinger. Works from this period reflect *Sturm und Drang* by portraying tremendous emotional upheaval, extremes of all kinds, and the struggle of the individual against social norms.

Monumentalism

This term applies to the late 19th-century tendency to create "monuments" of art that were epic in every sense of the word. In an effort to overwhelm in every way, large, long, oversized, powerful creative works appeared in every discipline.

Motive

An easily recognizable, repeating pattern in a work of art. In music, a motive uses a set of specific pitches and a distinct rhythm pattern.

Beethovenian/Beethoveniana

A term applied to all things concerning Beethoven, including works in the style of Beethoven's music.

DATES

1768:	Friedrich von Schiller writes a poem, part of which will become the text to the final movement of Beethoven's Symphony No. 9, Opus 125 (*Ode to Joy*).
1770:	**Beethoven's birth**
1776:	Friedrich von Klinger writes the novel *Sturm und Drang*. The American colonies declare independence from England. Thomas Paine publishes *Common Sense*.
1781:	William Herschel discovers Uranus.
1787:	**Beethoven travels to Vienna to meet Mozart.**
1789:	French Revolution begins.
1792:	**Beethoven arrives in Vienna.**

1802:	**Beethoven writes his *Heiligenstadt Testament.***
1803:	**Beethoven's Symphony No. 3 ("*Eroica*").**
	Thomas Jefferson makes the "Louisiana Purchase" from France.
1804:	Napoleon crowns himself Emperor of France.
1808:	**Beethoven's Symphony No. 6 ("*Pastoral*")**
1812:	America enters the War of 1812
1824:	**Beethoven's Symphony No. 9, Op. 125**
1827:	**Beethoven's death**
1828:	Andrew Jackson elected President of the United States

LISTENING

Ludwig van Beethoven	**Symphony No. 5 in C minor, Op. 67, Allegro con brio (1808)** (CD2/tr4)
	Symphony No. 6 in F major ("Pastoral"), Op. 68 (1808)
	Concerto No. 1 in C major, Op. 15, Rondo (1798) (CD2/tr5)
	Concerto for Violin in D major, Op. 61 (1806)
	Overture to *Fidelio,* Op. 72 (1804/1805/1814)
	"O welcher Lust" (Oh what Joy!) The Prisoner's Chorus. *Fidelio,* Op. 72 (1804/5/14)
	Piano Sonata in C-sharp minor ("Moonlight"), No. 14, Op. 27 (1801)
	Piano Sonata No. 18 in E-flat major ("Tempest"), Op. 31, No. 2 (1802)
	Piano Sonata No. 21 in C major ("Waldstein"), Op. 53 (1804)

String Quartet in E minor ("Razumovsky"), Op. 59, No. 2 (1806)

WEBSITES

http://www.bbc.co.uk/history/historic_figures/bonaparte_napoleon.shtml

A great place to begin learning about Napoleon and his military exploits.

http://www.napoleonbonaparte.nl/

Older students, or anyone interested in learning more details about a particular area of Napoleon's life, will enjoy using this site. It offers a guide to all the best Napoleonic websites, and would be especially helpful for those who want information on a certain topic, for instance, Napoleon's march into Russia or his exile.

http://artchive.com/artchive/F/friedrich.html

This site offers a biography of the artist Caspar David Friedrich and a synopsis of his work, his major influences, and those who were influenced by him. Because it is part of a larger online index of artists and artistic movements, the site features many helpful links to the other important artists or schools whose names appear in Friedrich's biography. It also includes a works list.

http://www.ibiblio.org/wm/paint/auth/friedrich/

A great site for younger students, this site offers a brief biographical sketch, with images of six of Friedrich's better-known works, which are discussed in the biographical section.

http://www.astroleague.org/al/obsclubs/herschel/fwhershs.html

This website tells the fascinating story of one of the fathers of modern astronomy, Sir William Herschel. You will be especially interested to read about the importance of music in his early life.

http://www.imagi-nation.com/moonstruck/clsc20.html

A wonderful introduction to Goethe's life and works, this site includes a number of helpful links to other Goethe-related sites on a variety of topics and levels. You will be surprised to learn about Goethe's interest in music and his scientific theories and research! Also view:

http://www.kirjasto.sci.fi/goethe.htm

http://www.lucare.com/immortal/index.html

Depending upon your prior knowledge of Beethoven's life, this site is either a thorough place for beginners, or a convenient place to begin research for more advanced students. The biographical portion is broken up into periods, focusing on his upbringing, his early career, and his later success and deafness. You will also find a number of helpful links.

http://www.naxos.com/composerinfo/Ludwig_van_Beethoven/25 976.htm

The official Naxos site on Beethoven, including biographical information, images, listening lists, and audio links. Also view:

http://www.sjsu.edu/beethoven
http://www.beethoven-haus-bonn.de
http://www.classical.net/music/comp.lst/beethoven.php

http://www.historycentral.com/1812/

A wonderful guide to one of America's "forgotten wars," this site is well organized and offers links not only to specific information about individual battles but to other wars as well.

PUTTING IT ALL TOGETHER

1.   Compare and contrast the French and American Revolutions. Consider the following points, including the French and American characteristics of each, and how/why those characteristics differ:

- Religious heritage
- Political traditions
- Day-to-day life for "ordinary" individuals
- Foreign allegiances/relationships

2.   Drawing on information from the other (earlier) units, select three compositions that would have been common during Beethoven's childhood (compositions composed around 1750-1775), and three compositions by other composers from 1820-1830. How do these differ in instrumentation, length, purpose or function, title, text, etc.?

3.   Spend some time researching the life and works of Goethe: although he is best known today for his significant contributions to German literature, he was very knowledgeable about and interested in other areas. What was his most important scientific theory? What kind of education did he receive, and for what profession? What kind of employment did he have during his lifetime (remember, writing did not always pay his bills!)? Were all of Goethe's works based on plots he developed, or were they based on other works? You may even want to research some of the

poets with whom he had close relationships. Create a smaller timeline that specifically parallels the major events of the American Revolution and Beethoven's life.

4.   A number of significant American figures, including Thomas Jefferson, John Adams, and Benjamin Franklin, spent significant time in Europe during Beethoven's lifetime. Do you think Beethoven would have been sympathetic to the American cause? Why or why not? Which men served as President during Beethoven's life?

5.   Research the Louisiana Purchase and the famous Lewis and Clark expedition: pay special attention to the wide variety of individuals who participated on the expedition. What kinds of things did Meriwether Lewis, especially, keep track of during the expedition? How do these things reflect the priorities of European culture during these years?

6.   Why did America fight the War of 1812? Was it a success for the United States? Where did most of the fighting take place? What effect did the war have on the city of Washington, D.C.? What happened to Napoleon in the first two years of the war?

VIEWING GUIDE

1.   Beethoven is famous not only for his music, but because

_____

_____.

2.   When the French Revolution broke out, Beethoven was _____ years old.

3.   Beethoven was the first significant composer to break away from

_____.

4.   Did Beethoven come from a musical family? _____.

5.   What kind of challenges did Beethoven face when he moved to Vienna at age 22? _____

_____

_____.

6.   Which celebrated, older author and thinker suggested some "polish" to Beethoven's personality? _____
Did it work? _____

7.   How did Beethoven respond to Napoleon? _____
_____
_____.

8.   What *kind* of opera was Beethoven's *Fidelio*?
_____. How many overtures did he write for the opera?
_____

9.   *Fidelio*, which was supposedly based on a true story, examined
realistic human themes including _____
_____
_____.

10.   As his deafness worsened, Beethoven's music became
_____.

11.   In Max Klinger's 1902 statue of Beethoven, the composer is
depicted as _____.

12.   How is Klinger's statue of Beethoven an example of 19th-century
monumentalism? _____
_____.

13.   The city of Heiligenstadt literally means _____.
Beethoven went there (why?) _____
_____. The strange letter he
wrote there in 1802 is called the Heiligenstadt _____ and
it's important in the study of Romanticism because _____
_____
_____.

14.   Parks in the 19th century change from _____
to _____.

15.   Particular features of Beethoven's music (especially when
contrasted with Mozart's!) include _____
_____
_____
_____.

16.   How did Beethoven change traditional tempo (and expression) markings? _____

_____ .

17.   We can see Beethoven's creative process in his many pages of musical _____ which have preserved _____

_____ .

18.   List some of the reasons why Caspar David Friedrich used the moon so much in his paintings. _____

_____ .

19.   William Herschel was known as the _____ , in part because he discovered _____ .

UNIT 11

SALONS, POETRY, AND THE POWER OF SONG

FIGURES

Johann Wilhelm von Goethe
(1749-1832)

Friedrich Schiller
(1759-1805)

Heinrich Heine
(1797-1856)

Alexander Pushkin
(1799-1837)

Lord George Byron
(1788-1824)

*John Keats
(1795-1821)

Percy Bysshe Shelley
(1792-1822)

Felix Mendelssohn
(1809-1847)

Fanny Mendelssohn Hensel
(1805-1847)

Franz Schubert
(1797-1828)

Carl Loewe
(1796-1869)

Robert Schumann
(1810-1856)

Clara Schumann
(1819-1896)

PLACES

Leipzig, Germany
Vienna, Austria

VOCABULARY

Lied
Pl. *Lieder.* German for "song," this term is also specifically used for art songs based on German poetry composed in the late 18th and 19th centuries.

Bourgeoisie
The social class between the aristocracy and the working class. We are likely to call it the "middle" class. Growth of the middle class, or *bourgeoisie,* was a phenomenon of great importance in Europe during the late 18th and 19th centuries. These people will become the newest patrons of music in the 19th century, purchasing tickets to concerts and operas, and buying instruments and music to play at home.

Gewandhaus (*Gewand*=garment/cloth) + (*Haus*=house)
This world-famous concert hall in Leipzig has been home to the celebrated Gewandhaus Orchestra for more than two centuries. The building was originally the home to Leipzig's fabric guild, until a group of Leipzig merchants founded a concert society and appropriated the hall for its use. The orchestra grew, and enjoyed many celebrated artistic directors, including Felix Mendelssohn. Today it is one of Europe's best orchestras.

Biedermeier
Originally a term used to describe a particular style of furniture popular in 19th-century Vienna, *Biedermeier* describes the clean lines and classical elements popular in all kinds of art and architecture between 1815 and 1848. These elements complemented a wider social phenomenon that focused upon home and family—the rising middle class—rather than nobility and privilege.

Ballad
This type of poem, a dramatic narrative featuring different characters and lots of action, was a frequent source of texts for *lieder.*

Erlkönig (*Erl*=Elf) + (*könig*=king)
This ballad, based on a Danish legend, was written in 1782 by Goethe, as part of a larger work, and subsequently set to music by a number of Romantic composers.

Liederkreis (*Lieder*=songs) + (*kreis*=circle, or cycle)
A group of related poems turned into songs, set into a specific order, and intended to be performed together.

Dichterliebe (*Dichter*=poet) + (*Liebe*=love)
From a large collection of poems by Heinrich Heine, sixteen poems were chosen by Robert Schumann and turned into a cycle of songs about disappointed love.

Salon
While a salon could be just a particular room in one's home, *salon* was also the term applied to a gathering of people or the artistic events that took place during the gathering. Guests would be invited on a regular basis, and the newest poetry and music would be the focus of the social event. Salons had varying social status, depending on whose home it was, which guests came, and who the featured artists would be.

Prima le parole, e dopo la musica
This Italian phrase translates, "First the words, and then the music," and it reminds us that both songs and dramatic vocal music (operas, oratorios, cantatas) begin with a text that forms the basis for the music.

DATES

1760-1820:	Reign of England's King George III
1829:	Louis Braille invents printing for the blind.
1834:	Indian Territory organized in the U.S.
1838:	Samuel Morse invents Morse Code.
1840:	**Robert and Clara Schumann are married.**
1845:	Elias Howe invents the sewing machine.
1854:	Henry David Thoreau's *Walden*
1855:	Walt Whitman's *Leaves of Grass*

LISTENING

Franz Schubert	***Erlkönig, Op. 1 D. 328 (1(1815)** (CD2/tr6)*
	Die Forelle (The Trout), D. 550 (1817)
	Heidenröslein (Little Heath Roses, or Heather), Op. 3, No. 3, D. 257
	Gretchen am Spinrade (Gretchen at the Spinning Wheel), Op. 2, D. 118 (1814)
	An Sylvia (Who is Sylvia? Text by Shakespeare), Op. 106, No. 4, D. 891 (1827)
Carl Loewe	***Erlkönig (1824)** (CD2/tr7)
Robert Schumann	***Dichterliebe, Op. 48 (1840)*** ***Im wunderschönen Monat Mai*** (CD2/tr8) ***Im Rhein, im heiligen Strome*** (CD2/tr9) ***Ich grolle nicht*** (CD2/tr10) ***Die alten, bösen Lieder*** (CD2/tr11) (try to hear the whole cycle!)
Felix Mendelssohn	Overture to *A Midsummer Night's Dream*, Op. 21 (1826)
	Octet in E-flat major, Op. 20 (1825)
	Venetian Boatsong No. 3, *Songs Without Words*, Op. 62, No. 5 (1844)
Fanny Mendelssohn-Hensel	Six Lieder, Op. 9 (published posthumously 1850)
Johannes Brahms	***Wiegenlied (Cradle Song) Op. 49, No. 4 (1868)*** (CD3/tr2)
	Wie Melodien zieht es mir (Like a melody, it pulls at me), Op. 105, No. 1 (1886)
Edvard Grieg	Six Poems by Henrik Ibsen, Op. 25 (1876)
Ernest Chausson	*Poème de l'amour et de la mer* (Poem of Love and the Sea), Op. 19 (1892)

Henri Duparc   *L'Invitation au voyage* (Invitation to a Journey)
                                (1872)

WEBSITES

http://www.imagi-nation.com/moonstruck/clsc20.html
By now you should know Goethe quite well; make sure that you have spent time at
the first site, then go on to find something new on the following sites:
http://www.kirjasto.sci.fi/goethe.htm
**http://www.aspirennies.com/private/SiteBody/Romance/Poetry/
Goethe/jwvgoethe.shtml**
http://www.theatrehistory.com/german/goethe013.html

http://www.kirjasto.sci.fi/hheine.htm
An introduction to the life and works of Heinrich Heine, one of the most popular
sources of text for *lieder*.
**http://www.poetryintranslation.com/PITBR/German/Heine.htm#
_Toc70244347**

http://halonine.tripod.com/pushkin.htm
An introduction to the life and wonderful works of Pushkin. Also view:
http://www.kirjasto.sci.fi/puskin.htm
http://www.pushkins-poems.com
http://poemsintranslation.blogspot.com/search/label/Pushkin

http://www.online-literature.com/byron/
If you have already become well acquainted with Byron's biography, take time to
read some of his poetry. More information and poems can be found on the following
sites:
http://englishhistory.net/byron.html
http://www.kirjasto.sci.fi/byron.htm
***NOTE: Due to information related to Byron's illicit "Romantic" lifestyle, the final
link may be unsuitable for younger students.***

http://englishhistory.net/keats.html
An introduction to the life and work of Keats, a "second generation" Romantic poet.
Also view:
http://www.john-keats.com/
http://www.kirjasto.sci.fi/jkeats.htm
http://www.online-literature.com/keats/

http://www.online-literature.com/shelley_percy/
An introduction to the life and works of Shelley, another celebrated Romantic poet who was friends with Keats and husband to Mary Shelley (author of *Frankenstein*). Also view:
http://terpconnect.umd.edu/~djb/shelley/home.html
Older students will want to view:
http://www.neuroticpoets.com/shelley/

http://www.naxos.com/composerinfo/Felix_Mendelssohn/24619. htm
The official Naxos website on Mendelssohn's life and work. If you are already familiar with this site, be sure to also visit the following:
http://www.classical.net/music/comp.lst/mendelssohn.php
http://www.balletmet.org/Notes/Mendelssohn.html

http://www.naxos.com/composerinfo/Franz_Schubert/21172.htm
The official Naxos site on Schubert, including biographical information, images, listening lists, and audio links. Also view:
http://www.classical.net/music/comp.lst/schubert.php

http://www.naxos.com/composerinfo/Robert_Schumann/24837.h tm
The official Naxos site on Schumann, including biographical information, images, listening lists, and audio links. Also view:
http://www.classical.net/music/comp.lst/schumann.php

http://www.naxos.com/composerinfo/Clara_Schumann/24836. htm
The official Naxos site on Clara Schumann, including biographical information, images, listening lists, and audio links. Also view:
http://www.dsokids.com/2001/dso.asp?PageID=448
http://www.pianosociety.com/cms/index.php?section=1350

PUTTING IT ALL TOGETHER

1.   Now that you've taken a peek into Mendelssohn's salon, consider some of the design elements that made it especially comfortable for musical performances. Compare its current organization as an "official concert space" in the Mendlessohnhaus Museum (chairs lined up in stiff rows, piano at the front) with the salon in Kupelweiser's painting of Schubert. Consider the differences—which salon

would be more suitable for a friendly gathering? Which seems more respectful to the performers? Which seems more appropriate for the early 19th century and why?

2.   Make a list of five of your favorite songs (remember: unlike a "piece" of music, *songs* require words). Consider the following:

-   What is the topic of the song? (What is it about?)
-   Where is the song *supposed* to be performed? (This may be difficult, since you most likely listened to this song on recorded media.)
-   If you've heard a live performance, where or how did the song differ from the recorded version?
-   If the song is accompanied, what kinds of instruments are used and how do they contribute?

3.   Consider how people interact with each other, and with the music, when they are gathered to listen to music in an informal, non-concert, setting. You may want to host a "salon" of your own, with some of your friends invited for an hour or two to listen to music and maybe have a snack.   Consider how the interests and personalities of the people affect the surroundings or the choice of music. Is it difficult "just" to listen to music without watching something or entertaining yourself in another way? How do you think the way you and your friends react is similar to, or different from, guests at a salon in the early 19th century?

4.   Visit the following website to learn more about Clara Wieck Schumann:

http://www.scils.rutgers.edu/~eversr/biogra2.html.

During the Schumann's concert tour to Russia in 1844, one of the guests at a reception honoring Clara tried to make polite conversation with Robert by asking him, "Are you musical as well?" If you had been there, and known Clara and Robert, what would have been your response to this question?

VIEWING GUIDE

1.   The _____ was the most popular stringed instrument during the "Elizabethan" era.   The Elizabethan Era was named for _____ who died in _____. The major author of that period was _____ and the most popular songwriter was named _____.

2.   According to Bob Falls, founder of *Poetry Alive!*, a simple definition of poetry would be _____

_____.

3.   Three requirements for optimal performance of a "good" song:

_____

_____

_____.

4.   Most songs benefit from a (size) _____ environment.

5.   Poetry can be performed in two ways: _____
or _____.

6.   List a few of the topics that were popular in poetry and song in the 19th century:

_____

_____

_____.

7.   During the 19th century, a *salon* was _____

_____

_____.

8.   These qualities are necessary to call a poem a ballad:

_____

_____.

9.   *In media res* means _____.

10.   In the ballad *Erlkönig,* the singer must convey the _____ (how many?) different characters in the story: (name them)

_____

_____.

11.   Song cycles, or *Liederkreis*, were "invented" during the (when?)
_____.

12.   Schumann was drawn to Heine's *Dichterliebe* in part because

_____

_____.

13. The first song of the cycle *Dichterliebe* is called "Im wunderschönen Monat Mai" and it is quite a happy song. This is noteworthy because _____

_____

_____.

14. There are moments of irony in this song cycle, including when the singer sings "Ich grolle nicht," which means _____.
But the composer (ironically) sets the words into music (how?)

_____

_____.

15. The final song, and the entire cycle, ends with _____

_____.

UNIT 12

A TALE OF FOUR VIRTUOSI
AND THE BIRTH OF THE TONE POEM

FIGURES

Nicolò Paganini
(1782-1840)

Franz Liszt
(1811-1886)

Frederick Chopin
(1810-1849)

Georges Sand (Aurore Dudevant)
(1804-1876)

Eugène Delacroix
(1798-1863)

Jean-Auguste Ingres
(1780-1867)

Jenny Lind
(1820-1887)

Moses Mendelssohn
(1729-1786)

Felix Mendelssohn- Bartholdy
(1809-1847)

Fanny Mendelssohn Hensel
(1805-1847)

Hector Berlioz
(1803-1869)

Vincenzo Bellini
(1801-1835)

John Field
(1782-1837)

PLACES

Genoa, Italy
Venice, Italy
Paris, France
Budapest, Hungary
Raiding, Hungary
Weimar, Germany
Leipzig, Germany
Warsaw, Poland

VOCABULARY

Etude
From *étudier*, the French verb meaning "to study." Within a musical context, an etude is a composition designed to exercise the player's ability to perform a certain skill or technical challenge on an instrument. Usually, etudes utilize that technical challenge in a much more difficult and exhausting way than ordinary pieces. Therefore, someone who can play the etude is better equipped to execute any ordinary piece successfully.

Character Piece
This is a very general category that includes all kinds of "little" instrumental pieces popular particularly during the 19th century. Chopin and his contemporaries, especially, composed literally hundreds of them for the piano. "Character Pieces" include the

> **Berceuse,** or lullaby
> **Nocturne,** or night piece
> **Barcarolle,** or boating song
> **Prelude,** which you will remember is often not a "prelude to" anything
> **Ballade,** or narrative style, free-form piece with direct opening
> **Rhapsody,** or free-form emotional piece
> **Intermezzo,** which gives the impression of connecting two larger works

Polonaise
Originally an ancient style of Polish national dance, Chopin made the Polonaise into a grand, virtuosic style piece for the piano.

Tone Poem (Symphonic Poem)

A composition for instruments, usually an orchestra or wind band, that seeks to describe a central theme, story, or emotion, using the language of music. Tone poems have titles and even "programs" or specific written outlines that give the details of the music's contents. Tone poems often rely upon *leading* or *guiding* motives to keep momentum going and to give a structure to the piece. Hector Berlioz is credited for the first Tone Poem, with his *Symphonie fantastique* in 1830, but Franz Liszt developed the idea methodically and richly, especially while living in Weimar from 1848 until 1861. He preferred to call his creations "Symphonic Poems." In the 19th century, tone poems were viewed as threatening to traditional symphonies and well-established musical forms. The debate over the tone poem was a large part of the "War of the Romantics."

Gewandhaus: (*Gewand*: garment) + (*Haus*: house)

This world-famous concert hall in Leipzig has been home to the celebrated Gewandhaus Orchestra for more than two centuries. The building was originally the home to Leipzig's fabric guild until a group of Leipzig merchants founded a concert society and appropriated the hall for its use. It was the home to many celebrated artistic directors, including Felix Mendelssohn.

DATES

1825:	Opening of the Erie Canal
1829:	**Mendelssohn conducts a revival of J.S. Bach's *St. Matthew Passion.***
1830-1831:	Revolution in Poland
1830:	**Berlioz composes his *Symphonie fantastique.***
1831:	**Liszt hears Paganini perform.**
	Cyrus McCormick invents the first commercial reaper.
1834:	Slavery abolished throughout the British Empire.
1835:	**Mendelssohn appointed conductor at the Leipzig *Gewandhaus.***
1836:	Battle of the Alamo
1837:	Samuel Morse invents the Telegraph.

1837-1901:   Queen Victoria rules the British Empire, the "Victorian" Era.

1840:   Friedrich Wilhelm IV crowned King of Prussia.

LISTENING

John Field   Nocturne in E-flat major, Op. 1, H. 24 (1812)

Frederick Chopin   Ballade in G minor, Op. 23, No. 1

                        Berceuse in D-flat major, Op. 57 (1835)
                        (CD2/tr14)

                        Etude ("Revolutionary"), Op. 10, No. 12
                        (CD2/tr13)

                        Polonaise in A-flat major, Op. 53 (1842)

                        Nocturne in C minor, Op. 48, No. 1 (1842)

                        Prelude in E minor, Op. 28, No. 4 (1839)

                        Prelude in D-flat major ("Raindrops"), Op. 28, No
                        15 (1839)

                        Barcarolle in F-sharp major, Op. 60 (1846)

                        Mazurka in B minor, Op. 33, No. 4 (1838)

                        Waltz in A-flat major, Op. 69, No. 1 (1835)

                        Scherzo in C-sharp minor, Op. 31, No. 3 (1839)

Vincenzo Bellini   "Casta Diva" *Norma* (1831)

Franz Liszt   ***Transcendental Etudes* No. 10 in F minor
                        "Appassionata" (1851)** (CD2/tr17)

                        Gnomenreigen (Dance of the Gnomes) *Études de
                        concert* (1863)

                        Hungarian Rhapsody, No. 2 (1847)

                        Mephisto Waltz No. 1 (1862)

	Symphonic Poem No. 2, *Tasso, Lamento e trionfo* (Tasso, Lament and Triumph) (1854)
	Symphonic Poem No. 5, *Prometheus* (1855)
Felix Mendelssohn	***Spinnerlied* (Spinning Song from Songs Without Words), Book 6, Op. 67, No. 34** (CD2/tr15)
	Piano Trio No. 1 in E major, Op. 1 (1839)
	Variations sérieuses (Serious Variations), Op. 54 (1841)
	Rondo Capriccioso in E-major, Op. 14 (1830)
Fanny Mendelssohn Hensel	*Das Jahr* (The Year), Suite for Piano (1841)
Nicolò Paganini	**Caprice in E major, Op. 1, No. 1 (1819)** (CD2/tr16)
	Caprice No. 24 in A minor, Op. 1 (1819)
Pablo Sarasate	*Carmen Fantasy* for violin, Op. 25 (1883)
Hector Berlioz	*Symphonie fantastique* (Fantastic Symphony: An Episode in the Life of an Artist) Op. 14 (1830)
John Williams	Film score to *Superman* (1978)
	Film score to *E.T.* (1982)
Edvard Grieg	***Peer Gynt* Suite No. 1, Op. 49** **Morning Mood** (CD3/tr7) **In the Hall of the Mountain King** (CD3/8)

WEBSITES

http://www.theviolinsite.com/composers/paganini.html

A brief, introductory biography of Paganini, with related links to other famous violin composers. Violin students, and string students in general, will wish to become familiar with this site, which offers a wealth of information on the instrument, from practice and audition tips to listening lists and video links.

http://www.paganini.com/nicolo/nicindex.htm

This site offers more detailed information about Paganini, including a broader family history and specific information related to his technical prowess on the violin.

http://www.naxos.com/composerinfo/Franz_Liszt/22599.htm

The official Naxos website on Liszt's life and works, including biographical information, images, listening lists, and audio links.

http://www.naxos.com/person/Franz_Liszt/22599.htm

This site offers more biographical information about Liszt, as well as an in-depth discussion of his compositions and how his compositional innovations influenced the works of others. Real fans of Liszt and his music will want to spend time at

http://www.classical.net/music/comp.lst/liszt.php. There you will

find a wealth of related links for those seeking more complete scholarly information.

http://www.naxos.com/composerinfo/Fryderyk_Chopin/25949.htm

The official Naxos website on Chopin's life and works, including biographical information, images, listening lists, and audio links.

NOTE: Even in these two websites, you will find a few different ways to translate Chopin's first name. Don't be confused—they are all for the same individual! Chopin is just one example of how the name of a composer changes appearance as it is translated from one language to another: in Chopin's case, from Polish, to French, to English, and then again from Polish directly into English!

http://www.answers.com/topic/george-sand

Although a notorious character in her day, Chopin's female companion, George Sand, was considered controversial in part because of practices that are now common for women, including wearing trousers.

NOTE: Parents should determine whether this site is appropriate for their student.

http://www.ibiblio.org/wm/paint/auth/delacroix/

Biographical information on the life and works of Delacroix, including a list of images. ***NOTE: Due to the violence and mature themes depicted in some of Delacroix' work, parents should determine whether this site is appropriate for their student, or select the links to those images that are important.***

http://www.ibiblio.org/wm/paint/auth/ingres/

Biographical information on the life and works of Ingres, including a list of images. ***Note: Due to Ingres' interest in the styles of Roman and Greek art, parents should determine whether this site is appropriate for their student, or select the links to those images that are important.***

http://www.americaslibrary.gov/aa/lind/aa_lind_subj.html
A brief narrative of Jenny Lind's journey to America and her rise as an international celebrity, geared towards younger students.

http://chnm.gmu.edu/lostmuseum/ (click on Jenny Lind)
A website dedicated to archives of Lind's trip to America, including press releases, reviews, and first-hand accounts of her performances.
http://www.lostmuseum.cuny.edu/archives/jlind.htm

http://plato.stanford.edu/entries/mendelssohn/
A biography of Moses Mendelssohn, including a brief narrative of his life and works as well as additional links to more detailed information for those interested in learning more about his influence on the German Enlightenment and his fusion of political theory and theology.

http://www.naxos.com/composerinfo/Felix_Mendelssohn/24619. htm
The official Naxos website on Mendelssohn's life and work, including biographical information, images, listening lists, and audio links. For more information, go to:
http://www.classical.net/music/comp.lst/mendelssohn.php

http://www.naxos.com/composerinfo/Fanny_Mendelssohn_Hense l/27352.htm
The official Naxos website on Fanny Mendelssohn-Hensel, including biographical information, images, listening lists, and audio links. For more information, go to:
http://www.essentialsofmusic.com/composer/hensel.html

http://www.naxos.com/composerinfo/Hector_Berlioz_25992/259 92.htm
The official Naxos website on Berlioz, including biographical information, images, listening lists, and audio links. For more information, go to the following sites, dedicated to Berlioz's life and compositions:
http://www.hberlioz.com/

http://www.naxos.com/composerinfo/Vincenzo_Bellini/25979. htm
The official Naxos website on Bellini, including biographical information, images, listening lists, and audio links.

http://www.naxos.com/composerinfo/John_Field/27167.htm

The official Naxos website on Field, including biographical information, images, listening lists, and audio links. For more information, go to:

http://www.nndb.com/people/439/000105124/

http://www.zum.de/whkmla/military/19cen/polishreb1830.html
A brief historical narrative of the 1830-1831 uprising of Poland against Russian occupation.

http://symphonysalon.blogspot.com/2005/12/franz-liszt-tone-poems.html
This website describes the characteristics of the symphonic, or tone, poem, its development in the mid 18th century, and its role particularly in Romantic music. The site includes a list of the best-known symphonic poems and the composers who used the tone poem most successfully. Also visit:

http://www.classical.net/music/recs/reviews/fenech/LisztSymPoem.php

PUTTING IT ALL TOGETHER

1.   In this unit, we have introduced you to some of "classical" music's most colorful celebrities—the virtuosi who captured the imagination of audiences in the 19th century. Because these composers lived and performed as famous individuals, we have lots of information available to tell us where and when they performed, what kinds of things they thought were important, what kind of friends they had, and what kinds of lives they led. Spend some time researching the life and compositions of each composer discussed in this unit. You may want to spend just enough time to get acquainted with each one, or you may already have a favorite on whom you want to focus. Be able to answer the following questions:

- What was this composer best known for in his or her lifetime: performing or composing?
- What other famous friends did s/he have?
- What important people did s/he meet or play for?
- Did s/he have other famous family members?
- Did s/he play other instruments?
- What other interests did s/he have?
- What was his or her upbringing like? How well educated was s/he?
- What did s/he read?
- Was this person wealthy?
- What things about the person's life surprise you?
- At what age did s/he die, and what was the cause?
- What past composers did s/he try to emulate?

2.   Throughout this course, we have focused on the three main sources of support for the arts: the church, royal courts, and the theater. Until the time of Beethoven, composers had to have some kind of job in one of these three places (and maybe more than one!) to survive. How did the virtuosi discussed in this chapter earn their livings? How, or with what, were they paid? How do you think the system for virtuoso performers has changed? How do they launch careers today? Where do they perform? How are they paid? How is their fame promoted?

3.   From Liszt's websites, and the website concerning the tone (symphonic) poem, what have you learned about this *genre*? Upon what are tone poems usually based? Do they have words (texts)? Where do tone poems usually get their names? Older students may wish to research the story behind one of their favorite tone poems.

4.   In this unit, the Mendelssohn family is unique because of the number of famous members who are discussed.   Research the three members of the Mendelssohn family. For what accomplishments was Moses Mendelssohn most famous? Why do we know Felix and Fanny by hyphenated names? What was the profession of Fanny's husband? Does this sound like a family you would like to be a part of? Why or why not?

5.   Today, we have a very clear idea of what a "concert" should be. What are some of the (many) differences you can think of between a contemporary concert (today) and concerts during the early 19th century? What would be fun about attending a concert in Liszt's or Paganini's day? How do these 19th-century concerts seem to have been different from performances with which Bach or Mozart would have been familiar?

6.   One kind of concert today is called a recital: this is essentially a concert where usually one or two players do all of the performing and receive all of the focus. Do some research and find a recital in your area: even if you cannot purchase tickets to hear the performance of someone well known or a recital in a fancy hall, you might be able to find recitals in the following locations. Many will be very inexpensive, or even free!

- Churches
- Community and senior centers (check your local paper)
- Libraries
- Local universities or colleges
- Museums
- Cultural centers

Develop a habit of regularly checking for performances in these locations. You will be amazed at what interesting concerts, recitals, and performance events take place!

7.   You may also wish to look at the concert and recital listings in a big metropolitan area (via newspapers or online). Check Chicago, New York, Los Angeles, Boston, for example. Figure out what is being performed when, and in what kind of hall. Try to find out who the "star" players are and what music they are performing. What would the tickets cost? If possible, follow up after the concert(s) by reading reviews that would be published in paper or online.

VIEWING GUIDE

1.   What do you think draws audiences to virtuoso musicians?
_____

2.   The first superstar virtuoso of the Romantic period was _____.

3.   What things about Paganini helped to make him famous?
_____
_____.

4.   The Romantic ideal considered art and artistic creativity to be
_____
_____.

5.   The young Paganini practiced his violin up to _____ hours per day!

6.   Another virtuoso who emulated Paganini was the pianist _____.

7.   Unlike Paganini, Liszt _____
_____.

8.   Liszt spent many grueling (if sometimes glamorous) years on stage as a _____ and he went virtually all over _____.

9.   While in Paris, Liszt's friends included _____, _____, and _____.

10.   During this time, what nickname did Paris gain? _____.
What had the Baroque King Louis XIV done to contribute to this

nickname? _____

_____ .

11. After Liszt left the stage, he went to _____ in order to _____ . Later, he moved to _____ so that he could _____ .

12. P.T. Barnum filled his circus acts with many "wonders of the world," including (from music) _____ such as the famous singer _____ from (country) _____ .

13. How was Chopin's music different from that of Liszt or Paganini?

_____

_____ .

14. The French verb *étudier* means_____ . An etude is

_____ .

15. Though he was (nationality) _____ born Chopin left his home at a young age to move to a much more exciting city, namely

_____ .

16. Did he ever return home? Yes ____ No _____

17. What is a "character piece"? _____

_____ .

18. Though Chopin is famous for his nocturnes, this kind of piece was invented by an (nationality) _____ composer and pianist named _____ .

19. Chopin is famous for his piano pieces. What kinds of works did he *not* compose? _____

_____ .

20. Although Felix Mendelssohn's family eventually became Protestants (Lutheran), his religion and ethnicity was

_____ .

21. Mendelssohn composed oratorios on what two famous Biblical stories? _____ and _____ .

22. Mendelssohn was also responsible for reviving interest in the compositions of one of our mega-composer, namely _____ .

23.   Mendelssohn was also an accomplished _____,
who recorded many scenes from his travels to Italy and Switzerland.

24.   Mendelssohn had a close relationship with his sister
_____, also an accomplished pianist and composer.

25.   Mendelssohn was one of the first persons to develop the role of
_____.

26.   Concerts in the early 19th century usually included _____
_____
_____.

27.   What are "Symphonic Poems" (Tone Poems)? _____
_____
_____.

28.   Who composed the *Symphonie fantastique*? _____.
What inspired the work? _____
_____.

29.   Liszt's followers called themselves the "Altenburg Eagles." What
was the "Altenburg"? _____

30.   As *Kapellmeister* in Weimar, Liszt was in a situation where
_____
_____.

31.   The troublesome genius-composer whose music Liszt
championed was named _____.

UNIT 13

NATIONALISM AND THE EXPLOSION OF ROMANTIC OPERA

FIGURES

Giacomo Meyerbeer
(1791-1864)

Carl Maria von Weber
(1786-1826)

Gioachino Rossini
(1792-1868)

Gaetano Donizetti
(1797-1848)

Vincenzo Bellini
(1801-1835)

Giuseppe Verdi
(1813-1901)

Giacomo Puccini
(1858-1924)

Georges Bizet
(1838-1875)

Sir Walter Scott
(1771-1832)

*Giuseppe Garibaldi
(1807-1882)

Otto von Bismarck
(1815-1898)

PLACES

Each "Place" in this unit is home to a famous opera house. Take time to visit the website of a few (or all!) of the following:

Paris:	http://www.operadeparis.fr/cns11/live/onp/site/
Venice:	http://www.teatrolafenice.it/
Dresden:	http://www.semperoper.de/en.html
Hamburg:	http://www.hamburgische-staatsoper.de/en/1_state_opera/
	hso/geschichte/index.php
Milan:	http://www.teatroallascala.org/en/index.html
Prague:	http://www.czechopera.cz/index.php?language=english
Sydney:	http://www.sydneyoperahouse.com/
Vienna:	http://www.wiener-staatsoper.at/Content.Node/home/
	Startseite-Content.en.php

VOCABULARY

Minuet
An early type of social dance (18th century) requiring the dancing couple to make physical, hand-to-hand, contact with one another. It has a triple meter, i.e. three beats per measure: 1-2-3, 1-2-3. Eventually, minuets became so common that many composers wrote pieces in the style of a minuet just for listening rather than for dancing.

Waltz
A later social dance that became popular in the late 18th century. It dominated the 19th century. The waltz was characterized by triple meter and the robust waltz *rhythm* found its way into many pieces of music in the 19th century, from operas to symphonies. Waltzing required more physical intimacy than the minuet, and was considered scandalous by some. Its high speed required the dancing couple to wrap their arms around each other and to lock eyes in order not to become dizzy.

Ballet
From the Italian verb *ballare*, which means "to dance." By the 19th century, ballet had become a highly disciplined, formal style of dancing intended for staged performance. Although most ballet performances now focus entirely on the dance, ballet first appeared as *intermezzi* between the acts of an opera or play. Ballet grew from Court Dancing. Dancing on the toe (for women), or *en pointe*, developed about 1830. Ballet in the 1830s and 1840s goes by the name Romantic Ballet. After the middle of the 19th century, an even more elaborate vocabulary of *en pointe* dancing became known as Classical Ballet. The Russians and the Danish became great masters of Classical Ballet.

Singspiel (*singen*=to sing) + (*spielen*=to play)
Singspiel is a form of dialogue opera in which the arias (songs) are sung while the information and dialogue (or conversation) is spoken. Unlike Italian opera, in which all of the story is sung throughout, whether in recitative or aria, the Germans found that their language worked best in opera if the dialogue were set in normal speech and the emotional parts (arias) were sung.

French Grand Opera
This style of opera was uniquely French in its grandeur. French "grand" operas were epic performances usually based upon sweeping and complex historical subjects. They always had five acts and tackled serious historical topics. They included at least one ballet (dance episode) and had big scenes for chorus. As a result, these beautiful and fascinating productions were (and are) incredibly expensive—one main reason these works are rarely performed. An example of French Grand Opera would be Meyerbeer's *Les Huguenots*.

Bel canto (*bel*=beautiful) + (*canto*=singing)
Although all opera is intended to be "sung beautifully," *bel canto* describes a specific kind of singing technique going all the way back to the 1600s. The term also refers to a type of operatic role in the 1700s and 1800s that emphasizes expression of the voice and ornate vocal melodies. *Bel canto* opera relies on a direct emotional appeal, rather than "grand" costumes, elaborate decorations, or historical weight. *Bel canto* opera can be serious or comic. An example of a comic *bel canto* opera would be Rossini's *Barber of Seville*, while a tragic one would be Bellini's *Norma*.

Risorgimento
Il Risorgimento (in Italian, *the Resurgence*) was the socio-political movement that led to the unification of the independent Italian states into one united nation called Italy. This long-overdue movement began during the end of Napoleon's rule and was concluded by 1871 (coinciding with the end of the Franco-Prussian War).

Verismo
A "realistic" approach to theater, including opera. *Verismo* opera is usually dark and tragic. Although the composer Puccini is most often credited with writing the finest *verismo* operas (*Tosca* and *Madame Butterfly*), Verdi decades earlier was incorporating quite a bit of realism, especially in his operas with tragic endings (*La Traviata*).

DATES

1815-1871:	Italian *Risorgimento*
1821:	**Weber's *Der Freischütz* has its premiere.**
1831:	***En pointe* dancing steals the show in Meyerbeer's *Robert le Diable.***
1852:	Harriet Beecher Stowe publishes *Uncle Tom's Cabin.*
1853:	***La Traviata* is premiered in Venice.**
1854:	Crimean War
	Kansas-Nebraska Act
1860:	South Carolina becomes first state to secede from the Union.
1861:	Italy is unified as one nation.
	Serfdom abolished in Russia.
1861-1865:	The American Civil War
1870-1871:	The Franco-Prussian War
1871:	Germany is unified as one nation.
	The Suez Canal is completed.
	Verdi's *Aida* is premiered in Cairo, Egypt.
1876:	Invention of the telephone
	Battle of the Little Bighorn
	First performance of Wagner's *Ring* in the *Festspielhaus* [see Unit 14]
1877:	**Invention of the gramophone**

LISTENING

Puccini	"Nessun dorma," *Turandot* (premiere 1926, left unfinished at composer's death in 1924) (CD3/tr12)
Bizet	Habañera, *Carmen* (1875) (CD2/tr12)

SELECTED VIEWING OF OPERAS AND BALLETS ON DVD

Puccini - *Turandot at the Forbidden City of Beijing,* conducted by Zubin Mehta. Maggio Musicale Fiorentino (1998)

A remarkable documentary, this DVD shows the construction of a production of *Turandot* at the great opera house of La Scala in Italy. It then was taken to the Forbidden City in China. A splendid way for the whole family to see how an opera is produced and to marvel at the resources China contributed to the production. The costumes and sets are blindingly beautiful. And there are interviews with the singers, directors, even officials involved in the delicate matter of transporting an Italian theatrical production to China.

Verdi. *Otello.* Directed by Franco Zefferelli. Teatro la Scala. Plácido Domingo and Katia Ricciarelli (1986)

This attractive *movie* version of Otello is smartly done with wonderful sets, realistic acting, and the fantastic voices of Placido Domingo and Katia Ricciarelli. In addition to being impressive as a film, it will provide an excellent basis for a comparison with Shakespeare's *Othello.*

Verdi. *La Traviata.* Directed by Franco Zefferelli. The Metropolitan Opera, conducted by James Levine. Plácido Domingo, Theresa Stratas (1983).

This heart-breaker is well done as a movie, with lovely sets. The opera is performed straight through (with subtitles, of course), and the movie-like aspect of it will capture the attention of those new to opera.

Adam. *Giselle.* Natalia Markarova, Mikhail Baryshnikov, American Ballet Theater (1992)

There are literally dozens of performances of *Giselle* available on DVD. This performance with Baryshnikov and Markarova is a classic, but you should try *several* productions for comparisons! Try any Russian production, especially the Kirov Ballet (Leningrad/St. Petersburg), or the 2008 production by the National Ballet of Paris, National Orchestra of Paris, 2008. There is an older performance that features legendary dancer Rudolph Nureyev, and while the video quality may not be as "modern," the dancing is phenomenal.

Bizet. *Carmen*. Directed by Carlos Saura with Antonio Gades (1983) Flamenco-Film Version.
A fascinating new way to look at *Carmen*, featuring the virtuoso dancing of Antonio Gades. Saura has created a story-within-a-story, in which a group of professional flamenco dancers are preparing a flamenco production of *Carmen*. Suddenly, a Carmen-like situation develops within the company. The principal parts of the opera are all heard, and the flamenco dancing is magnificent. Plus, you'll get an idea of how a dance production is rehearsed. There are gripping scenes, and viewers are likely to be entranced. Also, you can discuss how a story-within-a-story drama works. (There's a long tradition of this dramatic structure—start with a familiar one such as Shakespeare's *Hamlet*)

WEBSITES

http://classical-music-opera.com/
A wonderful classical music website; although the website focuses on opera, other links lead to information on concerti, masses, sonatas, and symphonies.

http://www.naxos.com/composerinfo/Giacomo_Meyerbeer/24631.htm
The official Naxos site on Meyerbeer, including biographical information, images, listening lists, and audio links. Also view:
http://www.meyerbeer.com/whois.htm

http://www.naxos.com/composerinfo/Carl_Maria_von_Weber/22404.htm
The official Naxos site on von Weber, including biographical information, images, listening lists, and audio links.

http://www.naxos.com/composerinfo/Gioachino_Rossini/26313.htm
The official Naxos website on Rossini, including biographical information, images, listening lists, and audio files. Also view:
http://www.classical.net/music/comp.lst/rossini.php

http://www.naxos.com/composerinfo/Gaetano_Donizetti/26004. htm
The official Naxos site on Donizetti, including biographical information, images, listening lists, and audio files. Also view:
http://www.donizettisociety.com/donizettilife.htm

http://www.donizettisociety.com/
This website provides information on Donizetti as well as a wide variety of people and artistic influences that were part of his era.

http://www.naxos.com/composerinfo/Vincenzo_Bellini/25979. htm
The official Naxos site on Bellini, including biographical information, images, listening lists, and audio links. Also view:
http://www.humanitiesweb.org/human.php?s=c&p=c&a=b&ID=1 13

http://www.naxos.com/composerinfo/Giuseppe_Verdi/21135.htm
The official Naxos site on Verdi, including biographical information, images, listening lists, and audio links.

http://www.naxos.com/composerinfo/Giacomo_Puccini/20991. htm
The official Naxos site on Puccini, including biographical information, images, listening lists, and audio links. Also view:
http://www.puccini.com/

http://www.naxos.com/composerinfo/Georges_Bizet/25998.htm
The official Naxos site on Bizet, including biographical information, images, listening lists, and audio links. Also view:
http://www.humanitiesweb.org/human.php?s=c&p=c&a=i&ID=53

http://www.online-literature.com/walter_scott/
A guide to the life and works of Sir Walter Scott, including quizzes on some of his most popular works. Also view:
http://www.lucidcafe.com/library/95aug/scott.html

PUTTING IT ALL TOGETHER

1.   Find a video or DVD copy of at least one of the operas on your listening list. Before you sit down to watch, spend some time at the composer's websites becoming familiar with the libretto and the background of the work and try to answer at least some of the following questions:

- In what year was this opera composed?
- How old was the composer in that year, and what was going on in his life?
- Is the opera set in the composer's home country? If not, why was the setting appropriate for the story?
- Was the story from a Biblical or literary source?
- How is this video production conceived? Is it like a stage production, a movie version, or a documentary? What do you find most engaging about this particular production?

Make sure you set the DVD to show English subtitles of what is being sung.

2.   Most of the world's great opera houses have their own websites that provide a wealth of information on what goes on "behind the curtain." Visit the website of each opera house, which you will find at the start of this unit in your list of "Places."

3.   If there is an opera company in your city or area, set up a field trip to view its rehearsal facilities. Most companies (even small ones) have a public relations liaison who will be happy to show you around and tell you or your group about their work. Here are some questions to get you started:

- How long is the company's "season," and how many productions are performed?
- Who decides which productions to perform?
- What is the budget for the entire season? For each production?
- Do they own the productions, or do they rent them (sets, costumes, etc.)
- How far in advance do they decide on the productions and book the singers?
- How old is this company? Has it changed over the years?
- What are the present goals of this company?
- What factors (economic, geographic, civic, artistic) are helping to shape the company's future?

4.   Take time to visit the website of each opera house listed in the "Places" section. These gorgeous buildings have equally gorgeous websites, so this will be a real pleasure! (If you need a little help with the foreign languages, look for the English translation button as necessary.) For each opera house, try to answer the following:

- In what year was the house built?
- Has it ever been destroyed and/or needed to be rebuilt? Remember: most of these buildings have existed through two World Wars, plus at least one national revolution!
- Does the house offer tours?
- How often do they offer performances?
- What is the price range for seating?
- Does the house offer "standing" places? Long lines of students and tourists almost always form, full of people willing to wait in line for hours just to stand through a full-length opera!
- Does the opera have any corporate sponsors?
- Do any non-opera groups use the house as well?

5.   Research the premieres of those operas listed in the "Dates" section. (The *premiere* is a work's very first public performance.) How well were the works liked? Why were the works commissioned? Who were the librettists?

VIEWING GUIDE

1.   Western ballet goes back to the court of _____. The biggest social-dance craze of the 18th century was the _____. Then, in the late 18th century, the _____ became popular, and it was more physically intimate and athletic.

2.   The word "ballet" comes from the Italian verb *ballare*, meaning

_____.

3.   About 1800, the German composer _____ wrote the first musical score specifically designed for a ballet.

4.   Ballet from the first half of the 19th century is known (stylistically) as _____, while ballet from the second half is known as _____. This is worth noting, because in music, the _____ style *precedes* the _____ period.

5.   Dancing *en pointe* was initially intended to depict _____

_____

_____.

6.   The first act of *Giselle* is based in the 18th-century (literary) world of _____, while the spooky second act is in the world of the_____. The female spirits wanting to gain revenge are called the _____.

7.   *Giselle* also had a _____ scene where the main character dances herself to death. This kind of scene became popular in the 19th century. There's an especially good one in Donizetti's opera _____, based on a novel by the popular English writer _____.

8.   A last point about *Giselle*: Adam uses themes called _____ to signify characters or objects. This will become common practice in 19th-century music.

9.   The (nationality) _____ greatly preferred to have much dancing in their (what kind?) _____ operas. They also liked visually extravagant scenes such as _____ _____ _____.

10.   An important theme in 19th-century opera is _____. Another "spiritual" theme important, particularly in German opera, is _____.

11.   German opera was changed forever in (date) _____ with a *Singspiel* called *Der Freischütz*, or "The Free Shot." This opera was especially popular with German audiences because _____ _____ _____.

12.   Germany did not become a united country until after the _____ in _____ (date). Italy did not become united until _____ (date).

13.   In America, we also like the *Singspiel* format, but we don't usually call it "opera." Rather, we call it a _____.

14.   What is the difference between an "ordinary" opera and a *Singspiel,* or "dialogue" opera? _____
_____.

15.   Do 19ᵗʰ-century operas depend upon a *lieto fine?* _____
_____.

16.   Who were the three greatest Italian opera composers in the first half of the 19th century (their names end in "i" ☺)? _____
_____
_____.

17.   *Bel canto* means literally _____
_____.

18.   Rossini excelled at many things, including writing excellent opening numbers called _____ and weaving the music and action   of   several   characters   together,   in   what   we   call
_____.

19.   Verdi's opera *Nabucco* tells the Biblical story of _____
_____. The famous chorus called
_____ is familiar to nearly every Italian, even today.

20.   What is a *scena ed aria?* _____
_____
_____.

21.   What was the *Risorgimento?* _____
_____
_____.

22.   *Viva Verdi* became a code for what revolutionary cry?
_____
_____.   Why was it necessary to put this seemingly innocent phrase   into   a   code? _____
_____
_____.

23.   What   culture   seemed   especially   exotic   to   the   French?
_____.

24.   Bizet's opera *Carmen* broke new ground because of the way it ended, namely _____. That kind of "realism" has a name in theater: _____.

25.   Radio broadcasts of _____, sponsored for decades by _____, were long a great source for listening to opera for people living outside of big cities.

UNIT 14

THE ABSOLUTELY NEW WORLD OF WAGNER

FIGURES

Richard Wagner
(1813-1883)

Franz Liszt
(1811-1886)

King Ludwig II
(1845-1886)

Friedrich Nietzsche
(1844-1900)

E. T. A. Hoffmann
(1776-1882)

Richard Strauss
(1864-1949)

PLACES
(dates in parenthesis refer to time when Wagner lived in these places)

Rhine River
Leipzig (birth city, 1813-1820; 1827-1831)
Dresden (1842-1849)
Wartburg Castle
Weimar
Zurich (1849-1861)
Vienna (1861-1864)
Munich (1864-1871)
Bayreuth (1871-1883)

VOCABULARY

Gesamtkunstwerk (*gesamt* = collected) + (*Kunst* = art) + (*Werk* = work)
"Total" or "Complete" art work; this term sums up Wagner's philosophy of how artistic productions should be conceived by the creator and consumed by the audience.

Das Kunstwerk der Zukunft (*Kunstwerk* = artwork) + (*der* = of the) + (*Zukunft* = future) "Artwork of the Future" (1849); the essay in which Wagner explains the idea of fusing music with staged drama, justifying his ideas by linking them to a legendary German past.

Leitmotiv (*leiten* = to guide, lead) + (*Motiv* = motive)
Guiding motives, used throughout Wagner's works to guide or lead the listener through his complex compositions; they can roughly be thought of as "theme music" or "signature themes" not only for characters but for major ideas, places, and concepts in the Ring cycle.

Festspielhaus (*Fest* = festival) + (*Spiel* = play) + (*Haus* = house)
The opera house designed by Wagner specifically for the performance of his works, especially the Ring cycle. Located in Bayreuth, in Bavaria (southern part of Germany), the *Festspielhaus* includes a number of structural and design elements that were revolutionary during Wagner's time; today most have become common elements of performance spaces.

Courtly Love
The Medieval ideal of relationships between men and women in which a man (a knight) sought the attention and support of his lady (typically a noblewoman). The legend of King Arthur and Guinevere is one example.

Minnesinger/Meistersinger
The Minnesinger (*Minnesänger*, pl.) was a 12th – 13th-century German poet-musician who crafted songs about the joys and follies of courtly love. These poets worked diligently to achieve the status of "master" (*Meister*) singers.

Novella
A fictional literary work, designated by its length; it is shorter than a full-length novel, but longer than a short story. A *musical novella* may use a musician as a principal character or use the power of music as a force in the plot.

Nibelungenlied
"Song of the Nibelung"; this epic poem, used by Wagner as part of the inspiration for the libretto of his Ring Cycle, dates from the early 13th century. Although typically credited to an anonymous German source, evidence also suggests that his version is actually a compilation incorporating even older, non-German legends.

National Socialism (*Nationalsozialismus*)
Commonly known today as Nazism, this political movement called National Socialism in English (an extreme form of Fascism) originated in Germany and was championed by Adolf Hitler.

Wagnerian (adj.)/ **Wagneriana** (noun, inanimate)/ **Wagnerian** (noun, animate)
General terms describing information pertaining to Wagner; can include anything from the substantial (such as lists of his works) to the trivial (anecdotes related to his descendents or family history). A "Wagnerian" is a person who *loves* Wagner's music.

DATES

1849:	**Wagner flees Dresden due to anti-government activity. *Das Kunstwerk der Zukunft* is published.**
1849:	Gold fever sweeps the United States.
1854:	The Kansas-Nebraska Act sparks a bitter controversy between "slave" and "free" states, beginning open hostilities that would lead to civil war.
1861:	**Wagner returns to Germany, sponsored by King Ludwig II.**
	Russian serfs are set free by decree under Tsar Alexander II.
1861-1865:	American Civil War
1862:	Homestead Act is passed in the U.S., beginning the great migration west.
1870-1871:	Franco-Prussian War
1876:	**First full performance of *The Ring* at the opening of the Bayreuth *Festspielhaus*.**

LISTENING

Discovering opera through selected brief listening tracks is like trying to teach a time-traveler about a new sport such as football by showing clips from a television commercial: it just isn't the same as growing up with sport, going to games, buying snacks, and cheering for your favorite team! This same problem affects Wagner's operas. There are hours of music from which to choose, but by now you have a sense of how Wagner would have felt about "only" listening to his music, without the experience of the theater and the scenery and the visual elements. Below are listed overtures and sections of Wagner's operas that have become popular in their own right; from there, feel free to venture out on your own!

Richard Wagner   Overture to *Tannhäuser* (1845)

Beglückt darf nun dich, the "Pilgrims' Chorus" from *Tannhäuser*, Act III

Overture to *Lohengrin* (1850)

Treulich gefuhrt ziehet dahin, the "Bridal Chorus" (Wedding March) from *Lohengrin*, Act III

***Vorspiel* (Prelude) from *Das Rheingold* (1869)** (CD2/tr18)

"Ride of the Valkyries" from *Die Walküre* (*The Valkyries*) (1870)

Overture to *Die Meistersinger von Nürnberg* (*The Mastersingers of Nuremberg*) (1868)

WEBSITES

http://www.bayreuther-festspiele.de/english/english_156.html
The official website of the ongoing Bayreuth Festival. Check out the seating for next summer. And the prices! (Remember to convert from Euros to dollars.)

http://www.wagneropera.net/Bayreuth/
An independent website documenting the history of the Bayreuth festival, including recordings, reviews, and a satellite photo of the *Bayreuther Festspielhaus*.

http://www.naxos.com/composerinfo/Richard_Wagner_22392/22 392.htm
The official Naxos site on Wagner, including biographical information, images, listening links, and audio files. Also view:
http://www.wagneroperas.com/

http://users.utu.fi/hansalmi/wagner.html
Website devoted to Wagneriana and Wagner-related research, maintained by one of the world's leading Wagner scholars.

http://www.ringdesnibelungen.com/index.html
Though not yet complete, this site documents an ongoing effort to create an animated version of the Ring.

http://www.musicwithease.com/wagner-ring-nibelung.html
Provides a synopsis of *Das Ring des Nibelungen*.

http://www.trell.org/wagner/motifs.html
http://well.com/user/woodman/singthing/ring/themusic.html
Guides to the *leitmotivs* of the Ring operas, complete with listening examples.

http://www.wagneroperas.com/indexwagneroperas.html
A concise guide to Wagner's thirteen completed operas, including cast lists, libretti, scores, and videos.

http://plato.stanford.edu/entries/nietzsche/
An introduction to the life and controversial works of Nietzsche, whose philosophies Wagner worshipped and adapted into his own writings. Also view:
http://www.kirjasto.sci.fi/nietzsch.htm

http://www.wagnermuseum.de/_engl/wahnfried/stage.html
Wahnfried – Wagner's home in Bayreuth.

PUTTING IT ALL TOGETHER

1.   There are many epic stories still popular today: Tolkein's *Lord of the Rings* trilogy, Lewis' *Chronicles of Narnia*, and even *Star Wars*, to name just a few. What makes a book or movie "epic"? Are you familiar with any epics (those listed above, or others)? What are the characteristics of a good epic? What makes them challenging?

2.   Watch one of these "epic" movies, or one of your own favorite movies, and pay close attention to how the music relates to the story. Are there specific melodies that seem to match certain characters? How does the soundtrack of the movie make dramatic, sad, or scary parts even *more* sad, dramatic, or scary? (If this is difficult to answer, watch the most intense "action" scenes with the volume turned all the way down so that you can't hear the music. Don't you find something is *missing*?)

3.   If you have never read the legend of King Arthur, find and read a literary version that is appropriate for you. You may be surprised to find a number of common story-telling elements – after all, they've been around a long time!

4.   Using the websites listed, do some research on the Bayreuth *Festspielhaus*. What do the design and architectural elements remind of you of? Who sings there nowadays? When are performances held? How much do tickets cost?

5.   Consider what was happening in the United States during the later part of Wagner's life. What other significant American historical events were taking place from 1860-1883? Using the information presented in the DVD and the biographical information you find on the Wagner websites, draw comparisons between the political unrest in which Wagner himself was involved in 1849 and the political unrest that was taking place in the United States.

VIEWING GUIDE

1.   The action in Wagner's *The Ring of the Nibelungs* is centered around the _____. These four operas are based on stories from _____ legends.

2.   Wagner's family background would be best described as _____.

3.   True or False: Hitler and Wagner were close, personal friends.

4.   Wagner became the musical "poster boy" for National Socialism because _____.

5.   Wagner's first fully successful opera _____ _____ was inspired, in part, by a real scare he had at sea when _____ _____.

6.   Wagner's experiences trying to "make it" in Paris were _____ _____.

7.   The _____ is the same castle where Martin Luther hid out in _____ (year) in order to _____ _____, and where the legendary Tannhäuser, centuries earlier, _____.

8.   Wagner came up with the term _____ to describe a work that incorporated all of the arts, with a single creator having complete artistic control.

9.   In exile, Wagner existed mostly on financial support from (person) _____, who did everything he could to keep people aware of Wagner's music.   Later, Wagner was financed by _____ who took the money from Bavaria's state budget!

10.   Perhaps Wagner's most famous idea was using a set of pitches called the _____ to represent the different _____ in his complicated opera plots.

11.   In Wagner's *Festspielhaus*, the orchestra pit is located largely _____ the stage.   Wagner designed it this way so that _____. Wagner even designed a new type of instrument, which we today call the _____.

12.   True or False: Wagner wanted people in his audience to relax, socialize, and simply enjoy themselves and have a good time.

13.   The complete *Ring* lasts approximately _____ hours! But it (circle one) was/was not intended to be seen in one long stretch.

14.   The only Wagner work on the Listening Set for *Discovering Music* is the Prelude (his name for Overture) to _____. Wagner would not have liked us to hear short excerpts from his operas because _____.

15.   True or False: It is easy for people to separate Wagner from Hitler and National Socialism (Fascism in the 1930s), especially today.

16.   True or False: The Wagner Festival at Bayreuth is a high-profile event still today.

UNIT 15

IMPERIAL RUSSIA – A CULTURAL ODYSSEY

FIGURES

Peter (Pyotr) Ilyich Tchaikovsky
(1840-1893)

Modest Mussorgsky
(1831-1889)

Sergei Rachmaninov
(1873-1943)

Dmitry Bortniansky
(1721-1825)

Mikhail Glinka
(1804-1857)

Nikolai Rimsky-Korsakov
(1844-1908)

*Mily Balakirev
(1837-1910)

*César Cui
(1835-1918)

Alexander (Akeksandr) Borodin
(1833-1887)

Alexander (Aleksandr) Scriabin
(1872-1915)

Igor Stravinsky
(1882-1971)

*Pope Leo IX
(1002-1054)

Alexei I
(1629-1676)

Peter the Great
(1672-1725)

Elizabeth I, Empress of Russia
(1709-1761)

Anton Chekov
(1860-1904)

Konstantin Stanislavsky
(1863-1938)

Alexander (Aleksandr) Pushkin
(1799-1837)

Ivan Turgenev
(1805-1883)

Nikolai Leskov
(1831-1895)

Leo (Lev) Tolstoy
(1821-1910)

Fedor (Fyodor) Dostoevsky
(1821-1881)

Sergei Diaghilev
(1872-1929)

Ilya Repin
(1844-1930)

***Vasily Surikov**
(1848-1916)

***Ivan Kramskoy**
(1837-1887)

PLACES

Constantinople (formerly Greek Byzantium, now Istanbul, Turkey)
Moscow, Russia
St. Petersburg (Leningrad/Petrograd), Russia
Kiev, Ukraine

VOCABULARY

Orthodox (*ortho*=right, or correct) + (*doxos*=bearer)
The name used to describe the Eastern Christian world with its spiritual center historically at Byzantium (Constantinople, today's Istanbul). The most holy Orthodox monastery is Mount Athos in Greece.

Serfdom
An ancient feudal practice that was maintained in Russian until 1861. Similar to slaves, serfs were essentially the members of society's lowest class of laborers. In Russia's vast rural economy, they were not legally free, but were bound to the land, to the Tsar (or other royalty), or to the Church, who essentially owned their labor and owed them only basic sustenance. Serfs had no control over their own lives, and had no rights beyond what their owners granted them.

Wanderers
Also known as the *Peredvizhniki* or the "Itinerants," this group of 19th-century Russian artists sought to portray life in Russia as realistically as possible. Their traveling exhibitions (which earned them the name of "wanderers") helped to raise awareness of poverty and illiteracy in Russia, as well as the plight of Russia's newly freed serfs. Prominent painters included Repin, Kramskoy, and Surikov.

Mighty Handful/Fistful
Also known as the *Moguchaia kuchka* or the "Mighty Five," this group of composers is considered responsible for developing a Russian school of composition. The main members of this group, which met in St. Petersburg from 1856-1870, included Balakirev, Rimsky-Korsakov, Mussorgsky, Cui, and Borodin.

Ballets russes
French for "Russian Ballet," this was the troupe of Russian dancers and artists assembled by Sergei Diaghilev for a long series of performance tours to Paris. By taking advantage of the French mania for dance and for anything Russian (and therefore "exotic"), Diaghilev was able to help young Russian artists, dancers, and composers gain international fame in Europe's most important cultural capitals. The productions were innovative, elaborate, expensive, and even scandalous.

DATES

988:	Prince Vladimir in Kiev (Ukraine) baptizes the *Rus* as Christians.
1453:	Orthodox Byzantium overtaken by Turks, Moscow becomes "Third Rome."
1825:	Decembrist Uprising
1830:	Pushkin's *Eugene Onegin* published.
1836:	**Glinka's *A Life for the Tsar* has its premiere.**
1861:	Tsar Alexander II abolishes serfdom.
1862:	**St. Petersburg Conservatory founded.**
1875-1876:	**Tchaikovsky tours the U.S.**
1892:	**Premiere of Tchaikovsky's *Nutcracker***
1910:	**Diaghilev's *Ballets russes* stages *The Firebird* in Paris.**
1911:	**Diaghilev's *Ballets russes* stages *Petrushka* in Paris.**
1913:	**Diaghilev's *Ballets russes* stages *Rite of Spring* in Paris.**
1917:	February and October (Bolshevik) Revolutions

LISTENING

Mikhail Glinka	*A Life for the Tsar* (1836) (may not be available on DVD)
	Overture to *Ruslan and Liudmilla* (1842) (DVD)
Nikolai Kedrov	***Otche nash* (Our Father, i.e. The Lord's Prayer) (CD3/tr3)**
Modest Mussorgsky	**"Promenade"(CD3/tr4) and "Ballet of the Chicks," *Pictures at an Exhibition* (1874) (CD3/tr5)**
	Night on Bald Mountain (Fantasy for Orchestra, 1886)

Peter Tchaikovsky	*1812* **Overture, Op. 49 (1882)** (CD3/tr6)
	Symphony No. 4 in F minor, Op. 36 (1878)

Recommended DVD Performances
Eugene Onegin. Metropolitan Opera (2007) Dmitri Hvorostovsky, Renée Fleming, conducted by Valery Gergiev

Swan Lake. Kirov Ballet (1999) Yulia Makhalina; Igor Zelinsky, conducted by Viktor Fedtov

Sleeping Beauty. The Royal Ballet (1995) Michael Somes, Beryl Grey, Margot Fonteyn, conducted by Robert Irving

Nutcracker. George Balanchine, New York City Ballet (1993). Narrated by Kevin Kline

Alexander Borodin	*On the Steppes of Central Asia* (Symphonic Poem, 1880)
	"Polovtsian" Dances, *Prince Igor* (1888)
Nikolai Rimsky-Korsakov	*Capriccio Espagnole*, Symphonic Suite, Op. 34 (1887)
	Sheherezade, Symphonic Suite, Op. 35 (1888)
Sergei Rachmaninov	Piano Concerto No. 2, Op. 18 (1908)
	Variations on a Theme of Paganini, Op. 43 (1934)
Alexander Scriabin	Etudes for Piano Op. 43, No. 5 (1905)
Igor Stravinsky	**"Danse infernale," *The Firebird* (1910)** (CD3/tr15)

WEBSITES

http://www.russianorthodoxchurch.ws/english
http://www.bbc.co.uk/religion/religions/christianity/subdivision s/easternorthodox_1.shtml
The Russian Orthodox Church

http://www.naxos.com/composerinfo/Pyotr_Il'yich_Tchaikovsky/
23876.htm
The official Naxos guide to Tchaikovsky, including biographical information and
images. Also view:
http://www.dsokids.com/2001/dso.asp?PageID=67
http://www.balletmet.org/Notes/Tchaikovsky.html
Older students, or Tchaikovsky fans of any age, will also wish to view:
http://www.tchaikovsky-research.net/en/

http://www.naxos.com/composerinfo/Modest_Petrovich_Mussorg
sky/20130.htm
The official Naxos site on Mussorgsky, including biographical information and
images. Also view:
http://www.dsokids.com/2001/dso.asp?PageID=292

http://www.naxos.com/composerinfo/Sergei_Rachmaninov_2100
1/21001.htm
The official Naxos site on Rachmaninov, including biographical information and
images. Also view:
http://www.classical.net/music/comp.lst/rachmaninoff.php

http://www.naxos.com/composerinfo/Mikhail_Ivanovich_Glinka/
26063.htm
The official Naxos site on Glinka, including biographical information and images.
Also view:
http://classical-composers.suite101.com/article.cfm/
composer_mikhail_glinka

http://www.naxos.com/composerinfo/Nikolay_Andreyevich_Rims
ky_Korsakov/26298.htm
The official Naxos site on Rimsky-Korsakov, including biographical information and
images. Also view:
http://www.russianlaw.net/RK/NARK.htm
http://www.classical.net/music/comp.lst/rimsky-korsakov.php

http://www.naxos.com/composerinfo/Alexander_Porfir'yevich_Bo
rodin/27086.htm
The official Naxos site on Borodin, including biographical information and images.
Also view:
http://www.classical.net/music/comp.lst/borodin.php

http://www.naxos.com/composerinfo/Alexander_Scriabin/24840. htm
The official Naxos site on Scriabin, including biographical information and images. Also view:
http://www.classical.net/music/comp.lst/scriabin.php
http://www.scriabinsociety.com/

http://prometheus.kai.ru/skriab_e.htm
Older students, or those particularly interested in Scriabin, will find this site fascinating: it offers a thorough explanation of Scriabin's theories on the synthesis of light and music. Because it is an English translation of a Russian site, it requires careful reading!

http://www.history-timelines.org.uk/places-timelines/36-russian-history-timeline.htm
Russia's history as a nation is a fascinating subject. An American student's knowledge of the subject is usually limited to some 20th-century Soviet history and perhaps the acquisition of Alaska by the United States. Here are some sources to help you get acquainted with this country's historical riches:
http://www.buzzle.com/articles/history-and-timeline-of-russian-czars.html
http://www2.sptimes.com/Treasures/TC.2.3.html

http://www.angelfire.com/pa/ImperialRussian/royalty/russia/russia01.html
A beautiful website with biographical information on the ruling members of the Romanov family, their palaces and residences, and a variety of other useful links. Information on individual rulers mentioned in this unit include:

http://www.angelfire.com/pa/ImperialRussian/royalty/russia/tsar02.html
An introduction to the life and times of Tsar Alexei (Romanov) I.
http://www.angelfire.com/pa/ImperialRussian/royalty/russia/tsar06.html
An introduction to the life and times of Peter "the Great."
http://www.angelfire.com/pa/ImperialRussian/royalty/russia/tsar11.html
An introduction to the life and times of Empress Elizabeth (Romanov).

http://www.online-literature.com/anton_chekhov/
An introduction to the life and works of Chekhov. Also view:
http://www.imagi-nation.com/moonstruck/clsc6.htm

http://people.brandeis.edu/~teuber/chekhovbio.html

http://max.mmlc.northwestern.edu/~mdenner/Drama/directors/stanislavsky.html
An introduction to the life and work of Stanislavsky, an important influence on theatre and cinema in the 20th century. Also view:
http://mhatschool.theatre.ru/en/international/

http://max.mmlc.northwestern.edu/~mdenner/Demo/poetpage/pushkin.html
Although you have probably explored the many links to Pushkin's biography in earlier units, take this opportunity to read a few of his shorter works in translation.

http://www.online-literature.com/turgenev/
An introduction to the life and works of Turgenev.
http://www.kirjasto.sci.fi/leskov.htm
An introduction to the life and works of Leskov.

http://www.online-literature.com/tolstoy/
An introduction to the life and works of one of Russia's greatest writer-philosophers, the author of *War and Peace*, *Anna Karenina*, and *The Kreutzer Sonata*. Also view:
http://www.kirjasto.sci.fi/ltolstoi.htm
http://www.biography.com/articles/Count-Leo-Nikolayevich-Tolstoy-9508518

http://www.online-literature.com/dostoevsky/
An introduction to the life and works of Dostoevsky.
http://www.kiosek.com/dostoevsky/contents.html

http://russianballethistory.com
An introduction to the Ballet Russe and the life and work of the great impresario Sergei Diaghilev.
http://www.answers.com/topic/sergei-diaghilev

http://www.abcgallery.com/R/repin/repin.html
A guide to the life and paintings of Repin. For more information on other members of "The Wanderers," and more classical Russian art, view:
http://www.allartclassic.com/author_biography.php?p_number=114
http://www.abcgallery.com/S/surikov/surikov.html

http://www.abcgallery.com/K/kramskoy/kramskoy.html

PUTTING IT ALL TOGETHER

1.   Select and view a video performance of one of Tchaikovsky's most popular and-best known ballets (see those suggested in Listening section above, or explore your own choices):

> *The Nutcracker*
> *Swan Lake*
> *Sleeping Beauty*

While you are watching, think about the following questions (you might want to take some notes), and answer them when the ballet is through:

- What aspects of the music help the dancers to make a transition from one scene to the next?
- How is dancing incorporated into the action of the ballet (which scenes involve a "dance" within the storyline)?
- How does Tchaikovsky's music set the mood in darker, spookier scenes? With a particular instrument, a silence, a change in tempo?
- How does the staging affect these same scenes? (Hint: You may want to watch some scenes with the volume muted so that you can focus on what is happening visually.)
- Research the plot: did Tchaikovsky write the original story?

2.   While learning about the lives of Tchaikovsky and the Mighty Handful, pay close attention to their early non-musical education. Were any of these composers trained for musical careers (as composers like Mozart or Haydn traditionally were)? If not, for which careers were they being prepared?

3.   Study the life of Chekhov, perhaps visiting the following link to read some of his short stories:

http://www.geocities.com/willemfh/chekhov.htm

What kind of early education and professional training did Chekhov receive and how does this remind you of the members of the Mighty Handful? What major political happenings took place in Russia during Chekhov's lifetime?

4.   Watch the film *Ivan the Terrible* (*Ivan Grozny*). This black-and-white film, made in 1944 and directed by famed director Sergei Eisenstein, offers a fascinating (and serious!) glimpse of the brilliant Soviet film director's approach to historical

subjects. The film was made at the height of World War II, and is laced with political meaning. Also, Eisenstein used film techniques far in advance of his time. What was Eisenstein's fate? (By the way, the film features a score by the great Soviet composer Sergei Prokofiev, who also wrote *Peter and the Wolf*.)

5.   Study the biographies of Tolstoy and Dostoevsky. What topics were their favorites? How did their personal backgrounds differ from the individuals about whom they wrote? What major political events happened in 1861? Did they write only "thick" (long!) novels, or did they also write short stories? Plays? What kind of religious beliefs did they hold?

6.   Study the final set of website links, which will take you to the paintings of "The Wanderers (Itinerants)." Carefully study their works depicting peasants. What kind of surroundings do you notice? What contrast do you see between the portraits of a single peasant and the ways in which peasants are depicted at work? Were these paintings completed before or after the liberation of the serfs in 1861? Take a moment to visit the website of the famous Tretyakov Gallery (in Moscow), one of Russia's most famous museums and permanent home to many of these works. **http://www.tretyakovgallery.ru/en/**

7.   Research the life and music of Sergei Rachmaninov. Try to understand his place in American musical life when he fled Russia after the 1917 Bolshevik Revolution. How did he seem to regard his new homeland? What happened to his career as a composer (in contrast to his career as a virtuoso pianist)? How has history judged his time in America? And what, generally, do people love so much about his music?

VIEWING GUIDE

1.   The principal key to understanding Russian music, indeed Russian culture, is to learn about _____.

2.   The very name Orthodox says a great deal, since the two roots are _____, meaning _____, and _____, meaning _____.

3.   The choral music in Russian Christian churches was (and still is) sung _____, which means "heads only" or unaccompanied. The melody lines were very (circle one) fluid / rigid.

4.   When Western-style music (and other ideas) entered Russian Orthodoxy in the 17ᵗʰ century, a group called the _____ rejected the new ideas and split off.

5.   Russian church music was characterized by low male voices and the rich sound of church _____.

6.   The religious images in Orthodox churches are called _____. It is important to understand that they are venerated, not _____. To venerate means _____ _____.

7.   Peter the Great was "great" in many ways, including his height, which was about _____ feet. He and his father started the trend of bringing in _____ musicians. Subsequent tsars, like _____, continued to do this.

8.   Bortniansky is considered the first really prominent Russian composer, but he was, in fact _____. This region was the _____ of Russian Orthodoxy in 988.

9.   Glinka is known as the _____. His opera *A Life for the Tsar* was so successful because _____ _____.

10.   The Russians kept the feudal system of _____ far longer than Europeans. It was abolished in (year) _____, but many problems still lingered.

11.   The Russian playwright _____ was very modern in his ability to probe the meaning of the small actions in our daily lives. His plays include _____. The theater director _____ created an entire method of _____ that explores this same psychology.

12.   In the mid 19th century, a group of painters known under several names, including _____ shocked people with their realistic paintings showing the poverty of the _____ and the arrogance of the _____. The most famous of these painters was named _____.

13.   Russia's most beloved author is named _____. His life bore striking resemblance to events in his greatest work, a novel in _____ called _____. While it's named after the

principal male character, the real hero of the story is _____.
The author himself died (how) _____.

14. Although people try to distinguish the composer _____ from a group of composers known as _____, they shared many of the same goals. But while _____ was committed to composing symphonies and concerti, the members of the other group were more interested in composing _____
_____.

15. The painter Viktor Hartmann, whose works are honored in the colorful piano cycle known as _____ died young. A repeating section called _____ links the musical portraits. A very scary Russian witch is portrayed, too, and she is known as _____. She "lives" in a hut that stands up on
_____.

16. The most famous Tsar in Russian opera has to be _____. He ruled during an *interregnum* or break between the _____ dynasty and the _____ dynasty. While it's still not clear what happened before he became tsar, he seems to have been troubled by a _____. Mussorgsky's operatic version has an extravagant _____ scene in the prologue.

17. In this opera, Mussorgsky seems to have found an important key to singing _____ in a natural and convincing way. There's also a wonderful _____ scene when the tsar sees a ghost of the murdered prince.

18. Biographers always note that Rimsky-Korsakov initially trained to be a _____. He was perhaps Russian music's best _____. He became a professor at the _____ _____ and despite his brilliance was always worried that he _____. Almost everyone has heard his piece called _____.

19. Late in life, Rimsky-Korsakov took an important student, one of his _____'s friends. This young man named _____ turned out to be one of the greatest Russian composers.

20.   Perhaps the most famous composer to flee Russia after the Bolshevik Revolution was _____. He came to _____ where he became _____ _____.

21.   Then there was the eccentric, and very modern Moscow composer named _____ who used unusual harmonies and was fascinated by _____. He explored this area by creating _____ _____. It could be considered "good" that he died before the _____, because its primary leader _____ would not have allowed the pursuit of such radical musical ideas.

22.   Sergei Diaghilev's theatrical troupe called _____ was a brilliant idea. He took _____ to the people who would most appreciate them, namely _____.

23.   The Russian composer _____ had many hits with the Ballets russes, including a ballet in 1910 about a magical creature called the _____ and another ballet in 1911 about a sad _____ named _____. The role of the puppet was danced by an amazing young Russian dancer named _____.

24.   There were actually two Russian _____ in 1917. The first in (month) _____ was a more-or-less democratic revolution. The second in (month) _____ is usually called the _____ and was led by _____ and had a drastic effect on Russian culture, namely _____ _____ _____.

UNIT 16

LOAD UP THE WAGONS: THE STORY OF AMERICAN MUSIC

FIGURES

Andrew Law
(1749-1821)

William Billings
(1746-1800)

Lowell Mason
(1792-1872)

John Philip Sousa
(1854-1932)

Charles Ives
(1874-1954)

Stephen Foster
(1826-1864)

Irving Berlin
(1888-1989)

Scott Joplin
(1867-1917)

Florenz Ziegfeld
(1867-1932)

PLACES

Old Salem, North Carolina
Bethlehem, Pennsylvania
New Orleans, Louisiana
Danbury, Connecticut
New York, New York
Boston, Massachusetts
San Francisco, California

VOCABULARY

Regionalism
This American phenomenon describes the different styles of music and means of music-making that sprouted across the continent throughout the nation's history. These styles have coexisted and continued into the present day, and are concentrated in different "regions" of the country.

Psalmody
This practice of composing and singing sacred music dates back to Renaissance England. As the name suggests, psalmody reflects a method of singing in which the melody was flexible and primarily reflected the meter of the Psalms of the Old Testament. The first book published in America was a book of Psalmody, the *Bay Psalm Book* published in 1640.

Hymnody
A general term describing the composition and singing of hymns.

Moravians
This group of Christians came from what is now the Czech Republic to Bethlehem, Pennsylvania, as missionaries, bringing with them European instruments and genres, as well as a love and respect for refined music and musical training.

Shape-Note Notation
This practice of writing the notes of the musical scale in different shapes made reading music more accessible to those who wanted to read music quickly and easily. Shape-note notation developed in the Southern United States and spread by way of traveling singing masters who would cross the frontiers establishing "singing schools" for a few weeks at a time. Famous early songbooks with shaped-note tunes included *Southern Harmony*, from 1835, and the *Sacred Harp* hymnal, from 1844. Quite a few of these tunes still appear in today's modern hymnals.

Handel and Haydn Oratorio Society
Established by a group of merchants in Boston, Massachusetts, in 1815, this choral society has survived to become one of the oldest continuously performing arts organizations in America. The Society produced the American premieres of such famous works as Handel's *Messiah* (in 1818), Haydn's *Creation* (in 1819), and J. S. Bach's *Mass in B-Minor* (in 1887).

Minstrelsy
Minstrelsy (Minstrel Shows) was a popular form of entertainment in the United States from the 1830s through the 1880s. Minstrel Shows were basically variety shows featuring songs, dancing, jokes, and vignettes by Caucasian performers in "black face" make-up. They mimicked the speech, movement, and vernacular of

African slaves on Southern plantations. Despite the gross injustices and distortions of the Minstrel Shows, this form of entertainment laid a foundation for American theater and entertainment that lasts until today.

Vaudeville

An American form of stage entertainment with roots in both Minstrelsy and European opera. Vaudeville swept America from the 1880s until the rise of "talking" movies in the late 1920s. Even then, the style of the Vaudeville show continued on to the big screen and eventually on television.

DATES

1730-1755:	First "Great Awakening," a series of American religious revivals
1770:	***The New England Psalm Singer* published.**
1790-1840:	Second "Great Awakening"
1815:	**Handel and Haydn Oratorio Society established, Boston, Massachusetts.**
1843:	**The Christy Minstrels established in New York City.**
1852:	*Uncle Tom's Cabin* published by Harriet Beecher Stowe.
1859:	**Opera House built in New Orleans, Louisiana.**
1866:	**Peabody Institute founded in Baltimore, Maryland.**
1883:	**Metropolitan Opera House built in New York City.**
1888:	**Birth of Irving Berlin**

LISTENING

William Billings	*When Jesus Wept* 1770
	Chester 1778
William Schuman	"Chester" from *New England Triptych* (a 20th-century setting of *Chester*) (1956)
Shape-Note Tunes	*O Wondrous Love* in *Southern Harmony* (1835) *Chester*
Scott Joplin	***Maple Leaf Rag* (1899)** (CD3/tr17)
	The Entertainer (1902)
Lowell Mason	*Joy to the World* (arr.)
	My Faith Looks Up to Thee
Charles Ives	***In Flanders Field* (1918)** (CD3/tr18)
	Variations on America (for organ solo) (1891)
	Symphony No. 3 ("Camp Meeting") (1904)
John Philip Sousa	*Stars and Stripes Forever* (1896)
	***Liberty Bell March* (1893)** (CD3/tr16)
	Washington Post March (1889)
Stephen Foster	*Oh! Susannah* (1848)
	De Camptown Races (1850)
	Ah! May the Red Rose Live Always (1850)
	Beautiful Dreamer (1864)
Civil War Era	*Marching Through Georgia* (Henry Clay Work, 1865)
	My Grandfather's Clock (Henry Clay Work, 1876)

Minstrel Tunes	*Old Dan Tucker* (c. 1830)
	Turkey in the Straw (a.k.a. *Zip Coon*, 1834)
Vaudeville Tunes	*My Mammy* (Walter Donaldson, 1921)
	April Showers (Louis Silvers, 1921)
Irving Berlin	*Alexander's Ragtime Band* (1911)
	A Pretty Girl Is Like a Melody (1919)
	God Bless America (1918)
Hans Zimmer	"Hakuna Matata" from *Lion King* (1994)

WEBSITES

***PARENTAL NOTE:** Remember that the historical information, texts, and images on some of these sites date back to a period of our nation's history characterized in part by racial divide and prejudice. To say that some of this material (specifically that from 1830-1880, or related to minstrelsy) is "politically incorrect" is putting it mildly. Please consider your student's age and understanding, as well as their ability to put certain words and images into historical context. ***

http://utc.iath.virginia.edu/minstrel/mihp.html
An online archive dedicated to minstrel memorabilia. This site includes images, playbills, historical reviews and advertisements, and even a digital enactment, of minstrel shows from 1830-1852. Playable audio files are included. Also view:

http://www.pbs.org/wgbh/amex/foster/sfeature/sf_minstrelsy. html
A wealth of information on the historical, cultural, and musical legacy of minstrelsy. Older students, or those interested in more advanced academic analysis, will want to view:
http://www.uncp.edu/home/canada/work/allam/17841865/music4.htm

http://www.amaranthpublishing.com/billings.htm
Information on the life, music, and writings of American composer and patriot William Billings, including links to sample MP3 files.

http://www.americanmusicpreservation.com/nema.htm

This site offers a collection of recordings and scores of American music from 1620-1920. Links to related American music websites are included.

http://www.cyberhymnal.org/bio/m/a/s/mason_l.htm
A guide to the life and work of Lowell Mason. Also view:
http://www.famousamericans.net/lowellmason/

http://www.naxos.com/person/John_Philip_Sousa_24864/24864.htm
The official Naxos site on Sousa, including biographical information and images. Also view:
http://www.americaslibrary.gov/aa/sousa/aa_sousa_subj.html
http://www.dws.org/sousa/

http://memory.loc.gov/ammem/amsshtml/amsshome.html
This site from the Library of Congress offers a wealth of American printed song sheets (many with illustrations). These songs were an early form of mass media and gave insight into the politics and social behavior of the Civil War Era.
http://lcweb2.loc.gov/diglib/ihas/html/civilwar/civilwar-home.html
This site from the Library of Congress offers a big collection of popular sheet music reflecting both sides of the Civil War. The song texts encompass issues from emancipation and reconstruction to military maneuvers. There are impressive illustrations plus many portraits.

http://www.charlesives.org/
The official site of the Charles Ives Society, including biographical information, works lists, and a number of helpful links. Also view:
http://www.naxos.com/person/Charles_Ives_24786/24786.htm

http://www.pitt.edu/~amerimus/foster.htm
A biography of Stephen Foster. Also view:
http://www.pbs.org/wgbh/amex/foster/
http://www.stephen-foster-songs.de/

http://parlorsongs.com/bios/berlin/iberlin.php
An introduction to the life and works of Irving Berlin. Also view:
http://www.rnh.com/irving_berlin.asp
http://www.jewishvirtuallibrary.org/jsource/biography/berlin.html

http://www.scottjoplin.org/biography.htm
An introduction of the life and works of Scott Joplin. Also view:
http://www.mostateparks.com/scottjoplin.htm
http://stlouis.missouri.org/501c/fsjoplin/

http://memory.loc.gov/ammem/vshtml/vshome.html
This site from the Library of Congress, entitled "The American Variety Stage: Vaudeville and Popular Entertainment 1870-1920," is a multi-media anthology of materials from this brilliant and formative era in American Culture, including playbills, motion pictures, play scripts.
http://memory.loc.gov/ammem/edhtml/edhome.html
This site from the Library of Congress includes a collection of early motion pictures and sound recordings from the Edison archive.
http://www.musicals101.com/ziegbio.htm
An introduction to the life of Florenz Ziegfeld and the history of the famous Ziegfeld Follies. Also view:
http://www.musicals101.com/ziegfeld.htm
http://parlorsongs.com/issues/2004-1/thismonth/feature.php

PUTTING IT ALL TOGETHER

1. Research the life of Stephen Foster. Be able to answer the following questions:

- What kind of musical education or training did he receive?
- Did he come from a family of musicians?
- Was he able to earn a living from writing his songs?
- What kinds of music did he compose?
- What effect did the Civil War have on his music? Did he compose any well-known Civil War songs?
- Did Foster write the texts (lyrics, words), or just the music to his songs?

2. Research the life and works of Scott Joplin:
- What "kind" of music did he make famous?
- Where is the Scott Joplin Ragtime Festival held? How often?
- Can we say for sure where and when Joplin was born?
- Who are the "Friends of Scott Joplin"? What do they do?

3. Research the history of local arts organizations in your town or neighborhood. These may include dance troupes, choral or chamber music societies, community bands, or large symphony orchestras. Who founded them? Back in the 1880s, it would have been a group of "society ladies"; today, it might be a group of like-minded folks in your suburb who want their communities to have

more offerings in the arts. Such groups are also founded by local professional musicians. But it nearly always comes back to individual persons and their bold visions. Here are some places to begin:

- the nearest orchestras, civic choruses, or opera companies
- art museums
- botanical gardens or zoos (these places often host outdoor performances)
- historical homes or villages
- libraries
- history museums
- retirement homes
- community centers
- churches or synagogues

When were these organizations founded? By whom? How was the money raised? How do they support themselves today? Who runs the organization(s) today? If you find an organization in which you are particularly interested, you may want to contact them to serve as a volunteer at a performance—hands are always needed for giving directions, handing out programs, answering questions, selling tickets, answering phones, or helping with refreshments!

4.   Discover the musical history of your hometown or region by trying to uncover any theaters or performing arts groups that served your community in the past. Working with your local librarian, historical society, or civic museum, you should be able to find out whether there were theaters in your town, vaudeville or minstrel performances, or musicales put on by professional or amateur groups. Maybe the circus came regularly through your area – does it still come through today?   What about orchestras, choruses, chamber music societies, opera and theater companies? Remember: developing some sort of "cultural" life or organization was often a crucial part of "settling" the west.   Even small towns without wealthy "society folks" put a high priority on bringing in some kind of cultural happenings because it would put them on the map. You might be very surprised at what you uncover!

5.   What was the history behind the name of New York's "New Amsterdam" Theater? How did it get this name? How is it related to the city's history? What unique feature did the New Amsterdam Theater have on its rooftop? Get a glimpse of the Theater by viewing:

http://web.bvu.edu/faculty/whitlatch/42nd/amsterdam.htm

VIEWING GUIDE

1.   Before anyone landed in America with a violin or a conductor's baton, there was _____

_____. While much of it has been lost because it was preserved mostly by _____ tradition, we still know that it fell into _____ such as songs for working, war songs, lullabies, dances, and songs for ceremonies.

2.   _____ means figuring out who settled where and brought which musical traditions with them.

3.   _____ were preserved up in the _____ Mountains in states like Virginia, West Virginia, and Tennessee. They have roots that go back to England, Ireland, and Scotland and were popularly used for dancing.

4.   San Gregorio de Abo is a mission located in what is today New Mexico. It was founded in _____ (date). Such missions were built to spread _____ and to teach _____ _____. The church music would have been sung in _____ (language).

5.   _____ was important in Colonial America. The tunes were carefully taught, and matched the words of the _____ from the Old Testament.

6.   The _____ were Czech missionaries sent to America. They started in Pennsylvania but many of them ended up in _____. These people valued European musical traditions. In Old Salem you can see an example of the kind of _____ built by an American instrument-builder named David Tannenberg.

7.   _____ singing is done enthusiastically today as a kind of musical hobby, the way quilting might be. But in the 19th century, it was the way _____

_____.

8.   Lowell Mason's most famous hymn tune (an arrangement) is an energetic Christmas Carol called _____.

But another famous hymn would be _____
_____.

9.   Sousa is known as the _____ King all over the world. People think of him in terms of his military band career, but he actually learned some of his showmanship from conducting _____.

10.   Many of America's artistic institutions, such as orchestras, opera companies, art museums, were actually founded by a group of _____ who organized everything, and then got their _____ to write the checks. These families became patrons of the arts, replacing the patronage of European _____ which we didn't have in America.

11.   An important institution in America, the _____ traveled from town to town, bringing wonders – from animal acts to opera singers.

12.   To get serious training, most American musicians had to travel to _____.

13.   The composer Charles Ives learned creativity from his father _____, who was the town _____. Ives is regarded today as the most significant American composer of his time, and yet, many of his friends and colleagues didn't _____.

14.   Charles Ives had an eclectic style, combing all kinds of melodies into his music, including _____
_____. He sent his friends copies of his _____ (which he paid out of his own pocket to publish), but he didn't get a very positive response. Today, these pieces are American treasures.

15.   The poem *In Flanders Field* was written by a _____ named John McCrae. You can see the influence of this poem every time you see someone wearing a _____ to honor _____.

16.   The festivities we call _____ in New Orleans are a direct result of American Regionalism because _____
_____.

New Orleans can also call itself America's _____ of Opera.

17.   On the West Coast, the musical and cultural influence of the _____ is of great importance. These folks were brought here to work on the _____.

18.   The first minstrel show was held in _____ (date); Minstrelsy was popular especially in the _____ parts of the United States. The actors wore what is called _____ made with burnt cork. We got many traditions of American entertainment from Minstrelsy, including _____ _____.

19. The   greatest   songwriter   of   the   Minstrel   Era   was _____. He's famous for songs like (choose one) _____. These tunes work well with an instrument called the _____.

20.   After the Civil War, the popularity of Minstrelsy (circle one) increased / decreased. Many of the features of Minstrel shows were kept   for   the   new   form   of   entertainment   called _____.

21.   One of the greatest (and longest-lived) American song writers of Vaudeville and Tin Pan Alley was _____. His family came from _____ to America. He (circle one) was / was not a highly   trained   musician.   His   first   smash   hit   was   called _____ in 1911.

22.   His music was also used as a theme song for a huge variety extravaganza called the _____ Follies. It found a home in the _____ Theater in New York. That theater was renovated in recent years by the _____ and had a gala opening with the musical _____.

UNIT 17

TURNING THE PAGE ON WESTERN TRADITION WITH THE EXPLOSION OF WAR

FIGURES

Johannes Brahms
(1833-1897)

Gustav Mahler
(1860-1911)

Alma Schindler Mahler Werfel
(1879-1964)

Richard Strauss
(1864-1949)

Arnold Schönberg (Schoenberg)
(1874-1951)

Edvard Munch
(1863-1944)

Gustav Klimt
(1862-1918)

Sigmund Freud
(1856-1939)

Claude-Achille Debussy
(1862-1918)

Charles Baudelaire
(1821-1867)

Stephane Mallarmé
(1842-1898)

Claude Monet
(1840-1926)

Edgar Degas
(1834-1917)

Paul Cezanne
(1839-1906)

Édouard Manet
(1832-1883)

Pierre-Auguste Renoir
(1841-1919)

Oscar Wilde
(1854-1900)

Bela Bartok
(1881-1945)

Zoltán Kodály
(1882-1967)

Sir William Schwenck Gilbert
(1836-1911)

Sir Arthur Sullivan
(1842-1900)

Kaiser Franz Joseph von Hapsburg
(1830-1916)

PLACES

Vienna, Austria
Paris, France
London, England
Hamburg, Germany
Budapest, Hungary
New York, New York

VOCABULARY

Fin-de-siécle (*Fin*=end) + (*de*=of) + (*siècle*=century)
A French term referring to the end of any century, but particularly to the years just before and after 1900. Like the phrase "turn of the century," *fin-de-siécle* includes the historical and cultural events that contributed to each unique historical setting—rather than just a set of dates.

Idiomatic
Any properties characteristic of the particular nature of something. For example: dialogue written in "bubbles" above a character's head could be considered "idiomatic" of a comic strip. Instrumental music that has been composed specifically to fit on a particular instrument is said to be "idiomatic."

Impressionism
A movement in art and music characteristic of *fin-de-siécle* France. Using delicate shadings and intricate blends of shape and color, visual artists sought to capture their "impression" of an image, rather than a concrete representation. The term was coined after an exhibit in 1874, in reference to Monet's painting *Impression: Sunrise* (1872). In music, it is often associated with the works of Debussy.

Symbolism
This aesthetic style encompasses a broad range of artistic "-isms" in many different countries throughout the 19th and first half of the 20th century. As the term suggests, *symbolism* simply involves using a symbol (for instance, a cross) to represent a person or idea, rather than discussing the person or idea directly.

Chinoiserie
The *fin-de-siécle* fascination with things Chinese and, by extension, anything Asian or "exotic."

Expressionism
Often confused with *impressionism*, this artistic movement arose in Germanic (Austria and Germany) nations at the turn of the last century. Expressionist artists sought to uncover the psychological "expressions" behind their images. The result is often darker and more severe than their Impressionist counterparts.

Sprechstimme (*sprechen*=*to speak*) + (*Stimme*=voice)
A vocal technique used by Arnold Schönberg, in works such as *Pierrot lunaire*, which combines singing and speech. In *Sprechstimme*, the performer strikes the note by singing it, and then lets the note decay (as one does when speaking) rather than sustaining the pitch. The result is intended to be surprising, perhaps eerie, and definitely expressive. Upon first hearing, it can be somewhat confusing to a listener.

Jugendstil (*Jugend*=youth) + (*Stil*=style)

More commonly known as *art nouveau*, this "youthful" style of art and architecture was an early 20th-century reaction to the overly ornate styles popular in the late 19th century. Called *Jugendstil* in German-speaking nations, *art nouveau* by the French, and *Art Deco* in America, this style was most commonly seen in such modern features as wallpaper, subway stations, wrought iron decoration, furniture, and jewelry. The famous firm Tiffany & Co. was a leader in creating this style.

Ringstrasse (Ring Street) + (*Strasse*=street)

Commonly called "the Ring," this wide boulevard runs through the heart of Vienna, Austria. The street traces the city's old garrison walls and marks the edge of the "old" and new parts of the city. Opened in 1860, the Ring is flanked on either side by museums, opera houses and theaters, public gardens, and luxury hotels and restaurants that reflect Vienna's opulent history as the cultural center of the Hapsburg Empire.

DATES

1851:	First World's Fair held in London.
1853-1856:	Russian-Crimean War
1860:	"The Ring" (*Ringstrasse*) opens in Vienna.
1870-1871:	Franco-Prussian War
1876:	**First Performance of Wagner's *Ring* in the *Festspielhaus***
1885:	Statue of Liberty arrives in New York City.
1889:	Eiffel Tower is built.
	North and South Dakota, Montana, and Washington admitted to the Union.
1890:	Oklahoma Territory organized.
1895:	Wilhelm Rontgen discovers X-Rays.
1903:	Wright Brothers' first airplane.
1914-1918:	World War I

LISTENING

Johannes Brahms	**Rhapsody in G minor, Op. 79, No. 2 (1879)** (CD3/tr1)
	***Wiegenlied* (Cradle Song), Op. 49, No. 4 (1868)** (CD3/tr2)
	Symphony No. 1 in C minor, Op. 68 (1876)
	Horn Trio in E-Flat major, Op. 40 (1865)
	Variations on a Theme by Haydn, Opus 56a (orchestral version) (1873)
Richard Strauss	***Don Quixote* (or, "Fantastic Variations on a Theme of Knightly Character), Op. 35 (1897). Thema – Knight of the Sorrowful Countenance** (CD3/tr9); **Variation II – Kriegerisch** (CD3/tr10)
	Dance of the Seven Veils, *Salome* (1905)
	Trio from Act III, *Der Rosenkavalier* (1911)
Arnold Schönberg	Overture to *Gurrelieder* (1900)
	Verklärte Nacht, Op. 4 (1899)
	Pierrot lunaire, Op. 21 (1912)
Gustav Mahler	***Ich bin der Welt abhanden gekommen* (*I have lost touch with the world*) (1902)** (CD3/tr13)
	Symphony No. 1 in D major ("Titan") (1889)
Claude Debussy	***Claire de lune* from *Suite Bergamasque* (1890)** (CD3/tr11)
	Prelude to the Afternoon of a Faun (*Prélude à l'après-midi d'un faune*) (1891)
	La Mer (*The Sea*) Three Symphonic Sketches (1905)
Giacomo Puccini	**"Nessun dorma," *Turandot*** (left incomplete in 1924) (CD3/tr12)

	La Bohème (1896)
	Madame Butterfly (1900)
	Tosca (1904)
Béla Bartók	*Allegro barbaro* for piano, Sz. 49 (1911)
	15 Hungarian Peasant Songs for piano, Sz. 71 (1918)
Gilbert & Sullivan	*Mikado* (1885) (DVD)
	Pirates of Penzanze (1879)
Igor Stravinsky	*Feu d'artifice* (*Fireworks,* tone poem) (1909)
	"Danse infernale," *Firebird* (ballet) (1910) (CD3/tr15)
	Petrushka (ballet) (1911)
	Rite of Spring (1913)
Charles Ives	***In Flanders Field*, S. 277 (1917)** (CD3/tr18)

WEBSITES

http://www.naxos.com/composerinfo/Johannes_Brahms/27097. htm
The official Naxos site on Brahms, including biographical information, images, listening lists, and audio links. Also visit:
http://www.johannesbrahms.org/
http://www.classical.net/music/comp.lst/brahms.php

http://www.naxos.com/composerinfo/Gustav_Mahler_22622/226 22.htm
The official Naxos site on Mahler, including biographical information, images, listening lists, and audio links. Also visit:
http://www.gustav-mahler.org/english/
http://www.classical.net/music/comp.lst/mahler.php

http://www.naxos.com/composerinfo/Richard_Strauss_26296/26 296.htm

The official Naxos site on Strauss, including biographical information, images, listening lists, and audio links. Also visit:

http://www.richard-strauss-festival.de/strauss/index. php?Set_ID=117
http://www.classical.net/music/comp.lst/straussr.php

http://www.naxos.com/composerinfo/Arnold_Schoenberg_21169/ 21169.htm
The official Naxos site on Schönberg, including biographical information, images, listening lists, and audio links. Also visit:
http://www.schoenberg.at/index.php?lang=en

http://www.edvard-munch.com/
The life and works of Edvard Munch; concentrate on the "Background" and "Gallery" sections, which will give you a thorough introduction to the Expressionist Movement as well.

http://www.expo-klimt.com/
An online gallery featuring one hundred of Klimt's works; also included is biographical information and a schedule of exhibitions. Also visit:
http://www.iklimt.com/
http://www.ibiblio.org/wm/paint/auth/klimt/
NOTE: Some paintings may feature images of the human body appropriate only for older students.

http://www.freudfile.org/
A guide to the life and research of Sigmund Freud, the "Father of Psychoanalysis" and the modern psychoanalytical movement. Also visit:
http://www.iep.utm.edu/f/freud.htm

http://www.naxos.com/composerinfo/Claude_Debussy_27153/27 153.htm
The official Naxos site on Debussy, including biographical information, images, listening lists, and audio files. Also visit:
http://www.essentialsofmusic.com/composer/debussy.html

http://www.poets.org/poet.php/prmPID/607
An introduction to the life and works of Baudelaire, including some excerpts.

http://www.kirjasto.sci.fi/mallarme.htm
An introduction to the life and works of Mallarmé.

http://www.ibiblio.org/wm/paint/auth/monet/
A thorough introduction to the life and works of Monet, including biographical information and many beautiful images. Also, be sure to view the following links for more information on Monet's time in Giverny:
http://giverny.org/monet/welcome.htm
http://www.abcgallery.com/M/monet/monet.html

http://www.ibiblio.org/wm/paint/auth/degas/
An introduction to the life and works of Degas. Also view:
http://www.ibiblio.org/wm/paint/auth/degas/ballet/
http://www.metmuseum.org/explore/degas/html/index.html
http://www.abcgallery.com/D/degas/degas.html

http://www.ibiblio.org/wm/paint/auth/cezanne/
An introduction to the life and works of Cézanne. Also view:
http://www.abcgallery.com/C/cezanne/cezanne.html
http://www.expo-cezanne.com/

http://www.ibiblio.org/wm/paint/auth/manet/
A guide to the life and works of Manet. Also view:
http://www.abcgallery.com/M/manet/manet.html
http://www.mystudios.com/manet/manet.html

http://www.expo-renoir.com/
A guide to the life and works of Renoir. Also view:
http://www.pierre-auguste-renoir.org/
http://www.abcgallery.com/R/renoir/renoir.html

http://www.oscarwildecollection.com/
An online resource for the works of Oscar Wilde. ***NOTE: This topic is most appropriate for older students.***

http://www.naxos.com/person/Bela_Bartok_25970/25970.htm The official Naxos site on Bartok, including biographical information, images, listening lists, and audio files. Also view:
http://www.boosey.com/composer/Bela+Bartok
http://www.classical.net/music/comp.lst/bartok.php

http://www.naxos.com/person/Zoltan_Kodaly_18828/18828.htm
The official Naxos site on Kodály, including biographical information, images, listening lists, and audio files. Also view:
http://www.boosey.com/composer/Zoltan+Kodaly

http://math.boisestate.edu/gas/
A well-organized and thorough source of information on the works of Arthur Sullivan and W.S. Gilbert, including some biographical information on the composers as individuals.

http://www.essential-architecture.com/STYLE/STY-Jugendstil.htm
An introduction to *Jugendstil* architecture.

http://www.macalester.edu/courses/geog61/aaron/
The history and architecture of the *Ringstrasse*, one of Europe's most famous and historic boulevards.

http://www.nps.gov/archive/stli/prod02.htm
Visit this site to learn about the Statue of Liberty.

PUTTING IT ALL TOGETHER

1.   Visit http://www.gustav-mahler.org/English, the official website of the International Gustav Mahler society. When was the Society founded, and for what purpose? What is the Golden Mahler-Medal, and to whom is it awarded? Also, click on the link to "Memorials" and read about these significant parts of Mahler's life and the works that they inspired. You will be surprised at how little these places have changed!

2.   Visit http://www.schoenberg.at, the official website of the Arnold Schönberg Center. What kind of things can you see and do at the center? Spend lots of time examining the links to the left, especially the top link ("Arnold Schönberg"). Look at the photographs from Schönberg's life and read about his philosophy and goals as a teacher. Did he have other talents aside from composition? Older students will want to read the "Essay," which places Schönberg's life and works in the broader context of contemporary music. By the way, both renderings of his name are correct: Schönberg and Schoenberg. Once he immigrated to America, he found the "oe" spelling easier to deal with.

3.   Study the works of the Impressionist artists, including Monet, Manet, Degas, Cézanne, and Renoir. Have you already seen some of these pictures? From reading

their biographical information, do you have a sense of which older artists influenced the younger ones? Did any of the artists have relationships with composers from our unit? When you have become familiar with the images from these artists, compare them to the Expressionist works of Munch and the *Jugendstil* works of Klimt: what general differences do you notice?

4.   Visit the following websites to learn about the purpose and history behind the World's Fair:

    http://www.expomuseum.com/history/
    http://jssgallery.org/essay/worlds_fairs/paris_exposition_1889/eiffel_
    tower.htm

Be sure to visit the links that give the fair's history from 1884-1916. What made the Eiffel Tower such a modern structure? What was unusual about it? How was it first received?

VIEWING GUIDE

1.   While _____ can mean the end of *any* century, it tends to mean the end of the _____ century.

2.   A phrase borrowed from the title of a book on culture in Vienna at the end of the 19th century, _____ describes the atmosphere rather well.

3.   Famous figures living in Vienna in the late 19th century included

_____.

4.   The massive building project on a street now called the _____ is a good symbol of the era, because

_____.

5.   A very famous Expressionist painting is entitled _____ by _____.

6.   Brahms is considered a Traditionalist because _____

_____

_____

_____.

7.   For some people, Brahms was the person who finally stepped out of the Shadow of _____.

8.   When music fits the instrument well, lies well in the player's hand, or the singer's voice, we call that kind of writing _____.

9.   Brahms' heart belonged only to one person, namely _____.

10.   Mahler was an intense composer. First, he was _____, so to get the job as conductor at the Vienna Royal Opera, he had to _____. He married a creative young woman named _____ who, herself, was a composer. After the marriage, Mahler wanted her to _____. The great tragedy in their lives was _____.

11.   Mahler's symphonies are revolutionary because _____
_____
_____
_____.

12.   Debussy is called the musician who rescued France from _____.

13.   While he did not like the term "_____ composer," Debussy is thought of that way because _____
_____. You could almost call Debussy a musical _____ because he had much in common with poets who used _____ as symbols.

14.   The painting after which the Impressionist movement was named is called _____ and was painted by _____. The word Impressionism (circle one) was / was not initially a compliment.

15.   The biggest musical influence sweeping across Europe at the end of the 19th century was _____.

16.   Puccini was a master at presenting realistic stories on the stage. He also knew the trends, such as a fashion for things exotic (Asian) called _____. His opera _____ uses an ancient Chinese fairy tale. Other popular operas involve stories people might recognize from the newspapers, such as _____.
But one of his greatest *verismo* (realistic) operas was a gorgeous but chilling work called *Tosca,* where the main character, an opera singer, both _____ the villain and (at the end) _____.

17.   People attended _____ to see exotic things and experience international culture and modern technology.

18.   _____ was a composer with two different musical lives. For decades he devoted himself to writing fantastic _____. But he also worked as a _____ and, starting around 1900, devoted himself to composing _____.
His 1905 shocker _____ still rivets audiences today.

19.   What is one clever way (in terms of set design) to provide water for a person singing the demanding role of Strauss' *Elektra*?
_____

20.   It's hard for us to realize just how amazed people were by the technology of _____ at the *fin-de-siècle.* People saw it mostly as a blessing that would sweep away the old inconveniences.

21.   Bartok found much of his inspiration by _____ _____ with a _____ in order to capture what he heard.

22.   Schönberg began his musical career writing music that was _____ in style. His piece for string sextet called _____ is a beautiful, dream-like piece. But soon, he began to leave Common Practice Era tonality behind, writing what is called _____ music. This was a very _____ thing to do. His audience (circle one) did / did not follow him happily.

23. Then Schönberg came up with a new way of _____ called *Sprechstimme.*

24. People talk about pre- and post- _____ ears because that ballet brought in many new things. Perhaps most innovative (and disturbing to many) was the _____, created by the brilliant Russian dancer _____. He had his dancers make movements that were _____

_____.

25. The important thing to do with music that is new, and challenging, is _____.

QUIZZES

UNIT 1: Using Music History to Unlock Western Culture

1.   If we learn what was happening when music was written, and what the music meant to the people who heard it, then we can create a _____ for the music.

2.   It's easier to absorb history if, everywhere you walk, you see _____ around you in daily life.

3.   For people immigrating to the United States, the key for success has been _____ languages, whereas the key for success in Europe has been_____.

4.   There's also a reverence for _____ in Europe, and people are more likely to quote _____ or make reference to them in regular daily life.

5.   Music is a funny term because in many languages it means _____ and not the _____.

6.   _____ means "work" in Latin.

7.   The length of a book's chapter depends on the kind of book and when it was written; similarly, the length of a _____ depends on what kind of music it is, and when it was written.

8.   Songs used to be any length, but after the invention of the _____, songs rather quickly became about _____ in length.

9.   Recorded music could last many minutes longer once the _____ became available. The initials mean

_____.

10.   Robert Schumann was not concerned about the length of his songs, but he did care about what (person) _____ thought about them! He was writing a lot of songs partly because _____

Unit 2: Music Entwined with Great Events in Western History

1.   The name of the castle where Martin Luther hid out and translated the New Testament into German: _____

2.   One of the earliest technologies for recording and replaying music: _____

3.   The scientific study of sound and hearing: _____

4.   This type of simple tune was used in the new Protestant (Lutheran) Church services: _____

5.   Inventor of the printing press: _____
When and where? _____

6.   In what year did the Reformation begin? _____
What does the word mean? _____. Who is the person credited with starting it? _____. What do we call the big branch of Christianity that came out of the Reformation?
_____

7.   This kind of printing using metal plates was originally developed by mapmakers: _____

8.   Printing music was more complicated than printing words because _____

9.   The district in New York City filled with music publishing houses where song-writers came, hoping to get their tunes published:
_____

10.   What was the purpose of the Council of Trent? _____
_____

UNIT 3: Technology, Terminology, and Cultural Perspective

1. _____ is all around us. We just have to look at things around us (buildings, objects), analyze them, and see the patterns of repetition and contrast.

2. A piece of instrumental music written for a large ensemble with separate movements may be called a _____. A genre of music involving four players (usually strings) is called a

_____.

3. The Italian word for speed (of a piece of music, in particular) is _____. The Italian word for "more" is _____, and for "less" is

_____.

4. A musical term meaning generally slower or "at ease": _____. A musical term for "quick":

_____.

5. Extraordinary performers who perform very difficult musical passages are known as _____.

6. The basic idea of opera goes back to _____.

7. This word, meaning a "kind" of music, comes from the Latin word "type" or "classification": _____.

8. A _____ is a 19ᵗʰ-century dance characterized by three beats or pulses per measure.

9. A _____ is a musical genre based on the Italian word *concertare*, meaning "to agree" or "to harmonize." By the time you get to the 19ᵗʰ century, the relationship between the soloist and the ensemble is _____.

10. The generic name (genre) given by a composer to a piece of music (circle one) does / does not tell you exactly what the music will be like.

UNIT 4: Fanfare and Power: The Court of Louis XIV

1.   Three institutions have supported the arts in Western Culture: _____, _____, and _____.

2.   Louis XIV was also known as _____.
Louis was very interested in fashion, including _____.

3.   What is a *faux pas*? _____. Dancing was more than a pastime. It was _____.

4.   Who was given the title of *Dauphin*? _____.

5.   What is the name of the most beautiful formal hall in Versailles? _____. Why did Louis XIV do so much to build up Versailles? _____

6.   When did Louis XIV reign? _____. How was he regarded by other monarchs who came after him? _____
_____.

7.   Charles Le Brun's paintings of _____ led King Louis XIV to take notice of the painter. Consequently, Le Brun became a _____ for Louis XIV.

8.   The most popular keyboard instrument of the era was the _____ _____. Why? _____

9.   What was Johannes Kepler's area of study and interest? _____. Another famous scientist of that time was _____.

10.   Who was Molière? _____.
What composer often worked with him to create wonderful productions? _____.

UNIT 5: Sweeping away the Renaissance into the Baroque

1.   A two-part structure in opera, the first conveying information and the second expressing emotion: _____ & _____.

2.   What is a *libretto?* _____. What is the root of the word? _____

3.   A musical texture involving a single line: _____. A musical texture involving several voices (or melodies) woven together: _____.

4.   Which dates encompass the Common Practice Era? _____ to _____.

5.   How many players are necessary to play *basso continuo?* _____. What kinds of instruments should be used? _____ _____.

6.   A word meaning "re-birth" that describes an historical era: _____.

7.   What do we call a composition that presents a melody, and then repeatedly imitates it, with contrasting episodes between these passages of imitation? _____

8.   *Opera* literally translates as _____. The first generally recognized opera (still produced today) is called _____ _____. Musicians love this Greek mythological story because _____

9.   Even tragic operas in the Baroque period were expected to end with a _____ (which means _____ ending).

10.   Which composer was among the very first to compose the new genre of opera? _____. What was he doing before he turned his talents to the new opera? _____

UNIT 6: Liturgical Calendar, Street Parties and the New Church Music

1.   Church celebrations during the year are recorded on a calendar we call the _____ calendar.

2.   The four weeks prior to Christmas Eve are known as _____. In the United States today, people tend to celebrate "Christmas" during these weeks, but that's because neither our daily lives nor our overall society is organized around the _____ _____.

3.   What are the sources for the plots (stories) used in most oratorios? _____.

4.   This genre of vocal music is based on the Italian verb "to sing": _____

5.   The long season of parties and feasting before Lent is known in Europe and South America primarily as _____ or in America as _____. How do people often dress at parties during this season? _____ _____.

6.   What are some names for the Tuesday celebrations right before Ash Wednesday? _____.

7.   Oratorios that tell the story of Christ's suffering leading up to his Crucifixion are called _____.

8.   Operas were appropriate for performance (circle one) before / during Lent? Why? _____. Oratorios were appropriate for performance (circle one) before / during Lent? Why? _____.

9.   Name two things you won't find in an oratorio that WOULD be found in an opera? _____ and _____

10.   Who was one of the greatest German Baroque composers of both opera and oratorio? _____. Which oratorio do most people know by this composer? _____

UNIT 7: A Lively Journey Through the Life of Johann Sebastian Bach

1.   A Baroque composer who lived and worked in Venice, Italy:

_____

2.   Even though most people don't do this, it would be better to use the middle name of Johann Sebastian Bach because _____ _____.

3.   This "Doctrine" reflects the Baroque idea of maintaining one musical style throughout a movement _____.

4.   *Sanssouci* was a _____ built by _____.

5.   One of Bach's older sons, _____, worked very successfully for Frederick the Great.

6.   Another of Bach's sons who was quite successful, J.C. Bach, is known as the _____ (city) Bach.

7.   What is meant by the "stations of Bach"? _____ _____. At which of Sebastian Bach's stations did he remain the longest? _____.

8.   What kind of young musicians did Bach supervise and teach? _____.

9.   In what new trendy spot did a lot of music-making take place in Bach's day? _____

10.   Name the notable German organist and composer whom Bach went hundreds of miles to see: _____. This story gets told a lot because Bach _____.

UNIT 8: Enlightenment, Classicism, and the Astonishing Mozart

1.   Who wrote an important treatise on the art of playing the violin?
_____

2.   Name one of the *Encyclopedists*: _____

3.   Which composer is known as the "Father of the Symphony"?
_____

4.   An early 18th-century French style that borrowed natural shapes such as pebbles, seashells, and vines: _____

5.   This long German term means "sensitive style":
_____

6.   This keyboard instrument was soft in sound, but very sensitive:
_____.

7.   An instrument named after the Italian terms for "loud" and "soft":
_____

8.   A term for light, funny 18th-century operas: _____.
Behind this style of entertainment lay an old tradition of Italian street and puppet theater called _____.

9.   Because this opera was a combination of funny and tragic, Mozart and his librettist _____ called
(name of opera) _____ a *drama giocoso,*
which means a _____.

10.   Haydn's greatest oratorio, _____, had a bilingual libretto in German and English.

UNIT 9: Into the Abyss: The Century Struggles with Unfettered Imagination

1.   The French soldier turned Emperor who attempted to conquer all of Europe, Britain, and Russia: _____

2.   The Greek philosopher _____ distinguished three levels of music: _____, _____ and
_____.

3.   An era that focuses on emotion, the individual, and the mysterious, rather than the balance and rationalism of the Enlightenment: _____

4.   A literary genre that became very popular during this period: _____. Shorter versions of this genre are called _____. A sub-category of this literary genre, where the story is conveyed by an exchange of letters, is called an _____.

5.   What kind of literature did the Brothers Grimm collect and publish? _____

6.   *Gemütlichkeit* could be described as _____.

7.   The author of *Ivanhoe*: _____. The author of *Frankenstein*: _____.

8.   The American Romantic poet who also embraced the supernatural and spooky: _____

9.   An author in Berlin who wrote short stories about fantastic events, many of them built around musicians: _____.

10.   Arguably the greatest Romantic author, _____, a German, became famous with an early book entitled _____ _____, a love story with a drastic ending. But his greatest creation was a play called _____ centered on a wager (a bet) between
_____
_____.

UNIT 10: Beethoven as Hero and Revolutionary

1.   Name the Romantic artist who painted many striking, even eerie, paintings of nature, especially the moon: _____

2.   Which French leader did Beethoven admire as a young man? _____

3.   What caused Beethoven to change his mind about this leader? _____

4.   What is the "Heiligenstadt Testament"? _____ _____

5.   To whom was this testament written, and for what reasons? _____ _____

6.   In music, what is a "motive"? _____ _____

7.   Name Beethoven's only opera: _____. What is one of its main themes? _____

8.   The 19th-century trend to create oversized "memorials" to great men in art, music, and culture is known as _____.

9.   What did William Herschel discover? _____

10.   We can learn a lot about Beethoven's actual note-by-note creative process because he left behind a lot of _____.

UNIT 11: Salons, Poetry, and the Power of the Song

1.   German for "song": _____

2.   In what social setting was "song" most often performed?_____
_____

3.   What style of furniture would you find in middle-class homes of this time? _____

4.   Which famous female composer was also sister to a composer and the wife of an artist? _____

5.   In which German city would you find the *Gewandhaus*? _____. What is it? _____
_____

6.   Which of the composers in this unit became the conductor and music director there? _____

7.   Name the famous German poet and thinker who wrote *Faust* but also wrote the text for many *lieder* (and he was friends with Beethoven):
_____

8.   What features distinguish a *ballad*? _____
_____

9.   _____, perhaps Romanticism's most famous *ballad*, was written by Goethe. It tells a story about a _____ child and was set to music by both Loewe and Schubert.

10.   _____ was a brilliant Viennese composer of song and symphony who died very young. Most of his career took place within the walls of aristocratic _____.

UNIT 12: A Tale of Four Virtuosi and the Birth of the Tone Poem

1.   Name the famous violinist who invented new playing techniques for his instrument in the early 19th century: _____

2.   Which famous pianist was inspired by seeing this violinist perform in 1831? _____ .

3.   Which famous Polish-born virtuoso composed almost all of his music for the piano only? _____

4.   What kind or style of piece is a "nocturne"? _____
_____

5.   Name a national dance from Poland: _____

6.   This kind of piece is meant as a "study": _____

7.   This French artist was a friend of Chopin and Georges Sand:
_____

8.   Who was the "Swedish Nightingale"? _____ .
What was her connection to the United States? _____ .

9.   Which French composer wrote the *Symphonie fantastique*?
_____ . What or who inspired him to do it?
_____

10.   What is a "tone poem"? _____
_____

UNIT 13: Nationalism and the Explosion of Romantic Opera

1.   This type of 19th-century opera involves a chorus, an historical plot, five acts, and lots of pageantry: _____

2.   What do we call the new style of dancing for women that, at first, was "spooky" but later became standard ballet technique? _____

3.   *Bel canto* literally means _____.

4.   What do we call the depiction of life and tragedy in a "realistic" way on stage, particularly in late 19th-century opera? _____
_____

5.   This kind of social dance from the 17th and early 18th centuries involved limited physical contact between the dancing partners:

_____

6.   This kind of social dance, popular throughout the whole 19th century, required holding on tightly, plus "locking eyes" to avoid dizziness: _____

7.   *Singspiel* literally means _____. We in America like to call this kind of operatic format a _____.

8.   This famous Italian operatic composer was hailed as a hero of *Il Risorgimento*: _____

9.   His ballet *Giselle* is a classic, but most people know Adolph Adam for a Christmas song called _____.

10.   The most famous early German Romantic opera by Weber is called: _____. What happens in the scariest scene? _____

UNIT 14: The Absolutely New World of Wagner

1.   Name the German king who supported Wagner's work financially.
_____

2.   Which German castle did Martin Luther "visit" and Wagner use as the setting for his opera *Tannhäuser*? _____

3.   *Gesamt=* _____, *kunst=* _____, *werk=* _____

4.   What is a *Leitmotiv*? _____
_____
_____

5.   What is a *Meistersinger*? _____

6.   What is the *Festspielhaus*? _____. Where is it located? _____. Why was it built? _____
_____

7.   Describe two special features of the *Festspielhaus*: _____
_____

8.   Which 20th-century dictator adopted Wagner's music for his own political use? _____

9.   Wagner wrote a lot of his essays and ideas for *The Ring* in (country) _____. He was there from 1849 until 1861 because _____.

10.   Which German river plays an important part in Wagner's operas?
_____

UNIT 15: Imperial Russia – A Cultural Odyssey

1.   Which Russian composer wrote *The Nutcracker*, as well as other famous ballets? _____

2.   *Orthodox* means _____.

3.   The Tsars loved to import their culture, and they were fond of appointing *Kapellmeisters* who were _____ (nationality). Finally, though, a native-born composer named _____ was appointed to this high post. He was not Russian, actually, but _____ (nationality).

4.   *Moguchaia kuchka* means _____. What kinds of jobs did the members of the *kuchka* have? _____

5.   The sound of _____ filled cities and villages. These important symbols of Russian Christianity and culture were destroyed during the _____Revolution of _____ (year).

6.   What was the *Ballets russes*? _____ _____ Where did they perform? _____

7.   Which early-19th century Russian composer is considered the "Father of Russian Music"? _____

8.   In the Christian church, what is an icon? _____ _____. In Eastern Christianity (Orthodoxy), an icon is not drawn or painted, but rather is _____; an icon is not viewed, or looked at, but is _____. And an icon is not worshipped, but is _____.

9.   What kind of themes did painters known as *The Wanderers* (*The Itinerants*) portray on canvas? _____ _____

10.   Which Russian city was called the "Third Rome"? _____

UNIT 16: Load Up the Wagons: The Story of American Music

1. What is "Hymnody"? _____
_____ Psalmody? _____
_____

2. Fiddle tunes come from what region? _____

3. How did Chinese music find its way to the West Coast of America?
_____

4. *Southern Harmony* and *Sacred Harp* were examples of what kind of notation: _____.

5. In which U.S. city was the first American opera house built?
_____

6. Which American composer, now famous for his symphonies and songs, worked as a pioneer in the insurance industry?
_____

7. Which American composer wrote American *Lieder* throughout the Civil War period? _____

8. For what genre of music is John Philip Sousa most famous?
_____

9. Old Salem, North Carolina was home to this group of music-loving missionaries from Eastern Europe (who first arrived in Bethlehem, Pennsylvania): _____

10. Which American theater entrepreneur made the New Amsterdam Theater famous? _____. What musical was staged to celebrate the recent renovation of this theater? _____

UNIT 17: Turning the Page on Western Tradition with the Explosion of War

1.   What time period is known as the *fin-de-siécle?* _____
_____

2.   Which composer developed *Sprechstimme?* _____

3.   Which composer represents, to us, the "Impressionist" movement? _____. Would he have liked our saying this? Yes / No

4.   Name two Impressionist painters: _____
_____

5.   Which artistic movement, the opposite of Impressionism, developed in Austria and Germany? _____

6.   In which city will you find the *Ringstrasse?*
_____

7.   What is *chinoiserie?* _____
_____

8.   What cataclysmic event began in 1914? _____

9.   Which German composer wrote a symphony considered to be "Beethoven's Tenth"? _____

10.   What is the name of the World War I poem that gave us the Red Poppy as a symbol of War Dead? _____

TEXTS AND TRANSLATIONS

CD 1, TRACK 1

FLOW MY TEARS
TEXT: ANONYMOUS (PROBABLY DOWLAND)

Flow, my tears, fall from your springs!
Exiled for ever, let me mourn;
Where night's black bird her sad infamy sings,
There let me live forlorn.

Down vain lights, shine you no more!
No nights are dark enough for those
That in despair their lost fortunes deplore.

Light doth but shame disclose.
Never may my woes be relieved,
Since pity is fled;
And tears and sighs and groans my weary days
Of all joys have deprived.

From the highest spire of contentment
My fortune is thrown;
And fear and grief and pain for my deserts
Are my hopes, since hope is gone.

Hark! you shadows that in darkness dwell,
Learn to contemn light
Happy, happy they that in hell
Feel not the world's despite.

DON GIOVANNI
TEXT: LORENZO DA PONTE

CD 2, TRACK 2
RECITATIVE: ALFIN SIAM LIBERATI

DON GIOVANNI
Alfin siam liberati, Zerlinetta gentil, da quel scioccone.
Che ne dite, mio ben, so far pulito?

ZERLINA
Signore, è mio marito. . .

DON GIOVANNI
Chi? Colui? Vi par che un onest'uomo, un nobil cavalier, com'io mi vanto, possa soffrir che quel visetto d'oro, quel viso inzuccherato da un bifolcaccio vil sia strapazzato?

ZERLINA
Ma, signore, io gli diedi parola di sposarlo.

DON GIOVANNI
Tal parola non vale un zero. Voi non siete fatta per essere paesana; un altra sorte vi procuran quegli occhi bricconcelli,
quei labretti sì belli, quelle dituccie candide e odorose, parmi toccar giuncata e fiutar rose.

ZERLINA
Ah! . . . Non vorrei . . .

DON GIOVANNI
Che non vorreste?

ZERLINA
Alfine ingannata restar. Io so che raro colle donne voi altri cavalieri siete onesti e sinceri.

DON GIOVANNI

DON GIOVANNI
At last we are free of him! That fellow clearly did not want to leave his Zerlinetta. Did I manage it well, my pretty daisy?

ZERLINA
My lord, he's my fiancé!

DON GIOVANNI
Who? That clown? You think a man of feeling, A well-born Cavalier, such as I am, can stand by quietly and watch such sweet and dainty freshness, such delicate perfections, all be thrown away upon such an insensitive rustic fellow?

ZERLINA
But, my Lord, I have promised to marry him tomorrow.

DON GIOVANNI
Who could help breaking such a promise? You were not intended by nature for a peasant; a brighter fortune is in store for those balmy cheeks of roses,
Where sly Cupid reposes, that delicate brow where not a shadow falls on it,
That pretty mouth of coral, that breathes of flowers.

ZERLINA
Ah, but I would not . . .

DON GIOVANNI
What is it that you would not?

ZERLINA
I am not about to be deceived. I know how seldom you great lords
Have honorable intentions with us simple country maids!

DON GIOVANNI

È un imposture della gente plebea! La nobiltà ha dipinta negli occhi l'onestà. Orsù, non perdiam tempo; in questo istante io ti voglio sposar.

That's a vile slander, a malicious invention; with noble birth, noble manners Always go hand in hand; I'll show you an example; This very instant I will make you my wife.

ZERLINA
Voi!

ZERLINA
You?

DON GIOVANNI
Certo, io.
Quel casinetto è mio: soli saremo e là, gioiello mio, ci sposeremo.

DON GIOVANNI
I, certainly: Come into my quiet house. Oh, come, my fairest angel, There I will marry thee.

CD 2, TRACK 3

DUET – LA CI DAREM LA MANO *DON GIOVANNI*

DON GIOVANNI
Là ci darem la mano,
là mi dirai di sì;
vedi, non è lontano,
partiam, ben mio, da qui.

DON GIOVANNI
Give me you hand, oh fairest,
Whisper a gentle 'Yes',
Come, if you care for me,
With joy my life to bless.

ZERLINA
Vorrei, e non vorrei,
mi trema un poco il cor,
felice, è ver, sarei,
ma può burlarmi ancor!

ZERLINA
I would, and yet I would not,
I dare not give assent,
Alas! I know I should not.
Too late, I may repent.

DON GIOVANNI
Vieni, mio bel diletto!

DON GIOVANNI
Come, dearest, let me guide thee.

ZERLINA
Mi fa pietà Masetto!

ZERLINA
Masetto sure will be angry with me!

DON GIOVANNI
Io cangierò tuo sorte!

DON GIOVANNI
Danger shall never be near you!

ZERLINA
Presto non son più forte!

ZERLINA
Ah . . . that I could refuse you!

DON GIOVANNI
Vieni! vieni!

DON GIOVANNI
Là ci darem la mano...

ZERLINA
Vorrei, e non vorrei....

DON GIOVANNI
Andiam! Andiam!

ZERLINA
Andiam!

DON GIOVANNI and ZERLINA
Andiam, andiam, mio bene,
a ristorar le pene
d'un' innocente amor!

ZERLINA and DON GIOVANNI
With you, with you, my treasure,
This life is nothing but pleasure,
My heart fondly belongs to you.

CD 2, TRACK 6 & 7

ERLKÖNIG
TEXT: JOHANN VON GOETHE

Wer reitet so spät durch Nacht und Wind?
Es ist der Vater mit seinem Kind;
Er hat den Knaben wohl in dem Arm,
Er faßt ihn sicher, er hält ihn warm.

"Mein Sohn, was birgst du so bang dein
Gesicht?"
"Siehst, Vater, du den Erlkönig nicht?
Den Erlenkönig mit Kron und Schweif?"
"Mein Sohn, es ist ein Nebelstreif"

"Du liebes Kind, komm, geh mit mir!
Gar schöne Spiele spiel ich mit dir;
Manch bunte Blumen sind an dem Strand,
Meine Mutter hat manch gülden Gewand."

"Mein Vater, mein Vater, und hörest du nicht,
Was Erlenkönig mir leise verspricht?"
"Sei ruhig, bleibe ruhig, mein Kind:
In dürren Blättern säuselt der Wind."

"Willst, feiner Knabe, du mit mir gehn?
Meine Töchter sollen dich warten schön;
Meine Töchter führen den nächtlichen Reihn
Und wiegen und tanzen und singen dich ein."

"Mein Vater, mein Vater, und siehst du nicht
dort
Erlkönigs Töchter am düstern Ort?"
"Mein Sohn, mein Sohn, ich seh es genau:
Es scheinen die alten Weiden so grau."

"Ich liebe dich, mich reizt deine schöne Gestalt;
Und bist du nicht willig, so brauch ich Gewalt."
"Mein Vater, mein Vater, jetzt faßt er mich an!
Erlkönig hat mir ein Leids getan!"

Dem Vater grauset's, er reitet geschwind,
Er hält in Armen das ächzende Kind,
Erreicht den Hof mit Müh' und Not:
In seinen Armen das Kind war tot.

Who rides by night thro' the woodland so wild?
It is the fond father embracing his child;
And close the boy nestles within his loved arm,
To hold himself fast, and to keep himself warm.

"O father, see yonder! see yonder!" he says;
"My boy, upon what dost thou fearfully gaze?"
"O, 'tis the Erl-King with his crown and his
shroud."
"No, my son, it is but a dark wreath of the cloud."

"O come and go with me, thou loveliest child;
By many a gay sport shall thy time be beguiled;
My mother keeps for thee many a fair toy,
And many a fine flower shall she pluck for my
boy."

"O father, my father, and did you not hear
The Erl-King whisper so low in my ear?"
"Be still, my heart's darling--my child, be at ease;
It was but the wild blast as it sung thro' the trees."

"O wilt thou go with me, thou loveliest boy?
My daughter shall tend thee with care and with
joy;
She shall bear thee so lightly thro' wet and thro'
wild,
And press thee, and kiss thee, and sing to my
child."

"O father, my father, and saw you not plain
The Erl-King's pale daughter glide past thro' the
rain?"
"Oh yes, my loved treasure, I knew it full soon;
It was the grey willow that danced to the moon."

"O come and go with me, no longer delay,
Or else, silly child, I will drag thee away."
"O father! O father! now, now, keep your hold,
The Erl-King has seized me -- his grasp is so cold!"

Sore trembled the father; he spurr'd thro' the
wild,
Clasping close to his bosom his shuddering child;
He reaches his dwelling in doubt and in dread,
But, clasp'd to his bosom, the infant was dead.

Translation: Sir Walter Scott

CD 2, TRACKS 8-11

FOUR SONGS FROM *DICHTERLIEBE*
TEXT: HEINRICH HEINE

In wunderschönen Monat Mai

Im wunderschönen Monat Mai,
Als alle Knospen sprangen,
Da ist in meinem Herzen
Die Liebe aufgegangen.

Im wunderschönen Monat Mai,
Als alle Vögel sangen,
Da hab' ich ihr gestanden
Mein Sehnen und Verlangen.

In Rhein, im schönen Strome

Im Rhein, im schönen Strome,
Da spiegelt sich in den Well'n
Mit seinem großen Dome
Das große, heil'ge Köln.

Im Dom da steht ein Bildnis,
Auf goldnem Leder gemalt;
In meines Lebens Wildnis
Hat's freundlich hineingestrahlt.

Es schweben Blumen und Eng'lein
Um unsre liebe Frau;
Die Augen, die Lippen, die Wänglein,
Die gleichen der Liebsten genau.

Ich grolle nicht
Ich grolle nicht, und wenn das Herz auch bricht,
Ewig verlor'nes Lieb! Ich grolle nicht.
Wie du auch strahlst in Diamantenpracht,
Es fällt kein Strahl in deines Herzens Nacht.
Das weiß ich längst.

Ich grolle nicht, und wenn das Herz auch bricht,
Ich sah dich ja im Traum,
Und sah die Nacht in deines Herzens Raum,
Und sah die Schlang', die dir am Herzen frißt,
Ich sah, mein Lieb, wie sehr du elend bist.

In the wonderfully beautiful month of May

In the wonderfully beautiful month of May
When all the buds are bursting open,
There, from my own heart,
Bursts forth my own love.

In the wonderfully beautiful month of May
When all the birds are singing,
So have I confessed to her
My yearning and my longing.

In the Rhine, in the holy stream

In the Rhine, in the holy stream
Is it mirrored in the waves -
With its great cathedral -
That great, holy city Cologne.

In the Cathedral stands an image
Painted on golden leather;
Into the wildness of my life
Has it shone, friendly.

Flowers and little cherubs hover
Around our beloved Lady;
The eyes, the lips, the cheeks -
They match my beloved's exactly.

I don't Complain (I bear no grudge)
I bear no grudge, even when my heart is
breaking!
Love lost forever! I bear no grudge.
Although you shine in diamond splendor,
No beam falls into the night of your heart.
I will know that for a long time.

I bear no grudge, and when my heart is breaking!
I truly saw you in my dreams
And saw the night in the room of your heart,
And saw the snake that bites your heart;
I saw, my dear, how truly miserable you are.

Die alten, bösen Lieder
Die alten, bösen Lieder,
Die Träume schlimm und arg,
Die laßt uns jetzt begraben,
Holt einen großen Sarg.

Hinein leg' ich gar manches,
Doch sag' ich noch nicht, was;
Der Sarg muß sein noch größer,
Wie's Heidelberger Faß.

Und holt eine Totenbahre,
Von Brettern fest und dick;
Auch muß sie sein noch länger,
Als wie zu Mainz die Brück'.

Und holt mir auch zwölf Riesen,
Die müssen noch stärker sein
Als wie der heil'ge Christoph
Im Dom zu Köln am Rhein.

Die sollen den Sarg forttragen,
Und senken ins Meer hinab;
Denn solchem großen Sarge
Gebührt ein großes Grab.

Wißt ihr, warum der Sarg wohl
So groß und schwer mag sein?
Ich legt' auch meine Liebe
Und meinen Schmerz hinein.

The Old, Angry Songs
The old, angry songs,
The dreams angry and wicked--
Let us now bury them.
Fetch a large coffin.

In it will I lay many things,
But I will still not say quite what.
The coffin must be still larger
As the cask in Heidelberg.

And fetch a death bier
And planks firm and thick;
They must be still longer
Than the bridge to Mainz.

And fetch me, too, twelve giants;
They must be still stronger
Than that strong St. Christopher
In the Cathedral to Cologne on the Rhine.

They should carry the coffin away
And sink it down deep in the sea,
Since such a great coffin
Deserves a great grave.

Do you know why the coffin
Must be so large and heavy?
I sank with it my love
And my pain, deep within.

Translations of songs from Dichterliebe: Paul Hindemith, D.M.A.
http://lyricbaritone.com

CD 2, TRACK 12

HABAÑERA *CARMEN*
TEXT: HENRI MEILHAC & LUDOVIC HALÉVY

L'amour est un oiseau rebelle
que nul ne peut apprivoiser,
et c'est bien en vain qu'on l'appelle,
s'il lui convient de refuser.
Rien n'y fait, menace ou prière,
l'un parle bien, l'autre se tait:
Et c'est l'autre que je préfère,
Il n'a rien dit mais il me plaît.
L'amour! L'amour! L'amour! L'amour!
L'amour est enfant de Bohème,
il n'a jamais, jamais connu de loi;
si tu ne m'aimes pas, je t'aime:
si je t'aime, prends garde à toi!

L'oiseau que tu croyais surprendre
battit de l'aile et s'envola . . .
l'amour est loin, tu peux l'attendre;
tu ne l'attends plus, il est là!
Tout autour de toi, vite, vite,
il vient, s'en va, puis il revient . . .
tu crois le tenir, il t'évite,
tu crois l'éviter, il te tient.
L'amour! L'amour! L'amour! L'amour!
L'amour est enfant de Bohème,
il n'a jamais, jamais connu de loi;
si tu ne m'aimes pas, je t'aime:
si je t'aime, prends garde à toi!

Love is a rebellious bird
that nobody can tame,
and you call him quite in vain
if it suits him not to come.
Nothing helps, neither threat nor prayer.
One man talks well, the other's mum;
it's the other one that I prefer.
He's silent but I like his looks.
Love! Love! Love! Love!
Love is a gypsy's child;
it has never, ever, known a law;
love me not, then I love you;
if I love you, you'd best beware! etc.

The bird you thought you had caught
beat its wings and flew away . . .
love stays away, you wait and wait;
when least expected, there it is!
All around you, swift, so swift, it comes,
it goes, and then returns . . .
you think you hold it fast, it flees
you think you're free, it holds you fast.
Love! Love! Love! Love!
Love is a gypsy's child,
it has never, ever, known a law;
love me not, then I love you;
if I love you, you'd best beware!

CD 3, TRACK 12

"NESSUN DORMA" FROM *TURANDOT*
TEXT: GIUSEPPE ADAMI & RENATO SIMONI

Nessun dorma!	No man shall sleep! No man shall sleep!
Tu pure, o Principessa,	You too, o Princess,
nella tua fredda stanza	in your chaste room
guardi le stelle che tremano	are watching the stars which
d'amore e di speranza!	tremble with love and hope!
Ma il mio mistero è chiuso in me,	But my secret lies hidden within me,
il nome mio nessun saprà!	no one shall discover my name!
No, no, sulla tua bocca lo dirò,	Oh no, I will reveal it only on your lips,
quando la luce splenderà!	when daylight shines forth
Ed il mio bacio scioglierà	and my kiss shall break
il silenzio che ti fa mia!	the silence which makes you mine!

CD 3, TRACK 13

ICH BIN DER WELT ABHANDEN GEKOMMEN
TEXT: FRIEDRICH RÜCKERT

Ich bin der Welt abhanden gekommen,	I am lost to the world
Mit der ich sonst viele Zeit verdorben,	with which I used to waste so much time,
Sie hat so lange nichts von mir vernommen,	It has heard nothing from me for so long
Sie mag wohl glauben, ich sei gestorben!	that it may very well believe that I am dead!
Es ist mir auch gar nichts daran gelegen,	It is of no consequence to me
Ob sie mich für gestorben hält,	Whether it thinks me dead;
Ich kann auch gar nichts sagen dagegen,	I cannot deny it,
Denn wirklich bin ich gestorben der Welt.	for I really am dead to the world.
Ich bin gestorben dem Weltgetümmel,	I am dead to the world's tumult,
Und ruh' in einem stillen Gebiet!	And I rest in a quiet realm!
Ich leb' allein in meinem Himmel,	I live alone in my heaven,
In meinem Lieben, in meinem Lied!	In my love and in my song!

Translation: Emily Ezust, http://www.recmusic.org/lieder/

CD 3, TRACK 14

THE CALL
TEXT: GEORGE HERBERT

Come, my Way, my Truth, my Life:
Such a Way, as gives us breath:
Such a Truth, as ends all strife:
Such a Life, as killeth death.

Come, My Light, my Feast, my Strength:
Such a Light, as shows a feast:
Such a Feast, as mends in length:
Such a Strength, as makes his guest.

Come, my Joy, my Love, my Heart:
Such a Joy, as none can move:
Such a Love, as none can part:
Such a Heart, as joys in love.

CD 3, TRACK 18

IN FLANDERS FIELD
TEXT: LT. COL JOHN MCCRAE

In Flanders Field the poppies blow
Between the crosses row on row,
That mark our place; and in the sky
The larks, still bravely singing fly.
Scarce heard amid the guns below.

We are the Dead. Short days ago
We lived, felt dawn, saw sunset glow.
Loved and were loved,
And now we lie
In Flanders Field.

Take up our quarrel with the foe:
To you from falling hands we throw
The torch; be yours to hold it high.
If ye break faith with us who die
We shall not sleep, though poppies grow
In Flanders Field

ANSWER KEY FOR QUIZZES

A semicolon (;) is used to separate answers. A slash (/) separates variant (possible or suggested) answers. More than one answer can be correct in many cases.

Unit 1: Using Music History to Unlock Western Culture
1. cultural context / an example or piece of music history
2. monuments / historical buildings / historical plaques
3. eliminating / leaving behind ; learning multiple languages
4. literature; writers / authors / novels / poems
5. sound only ; written notes on a page (i.e., the score)
6. opus
7. movement
8. gramophone ; 3 minutes (on a gramophone cylinder or disc)
9. LP ; Long-Playing
10. Clara (Wieck) ; they were in love / they were seeking permission to get married.

Unit 2: Music Entwined with Great Events in Western History
1. Wartburg Castle
2. gramophone
3. acoustics
4. chorale / hymn
5. Gutenberg ; c. 1450 ; Mainz, Germany
6. 1517 ; to reform ; Martin Luther ; Protestant
7. engraving
8. There were so many small symbols to print, and they had to be placed correctly on the musical lines (staff). Then the words (text) had to be put in too. It took multiple impressions.
9. Tin Pan Alley
10. to combat what they saw as the mistakes of the new Protestant denominations (Lutherans) and to create new, more accessible and more attractive elements of worship.

Unit 3: Technology, Terminology, and Cultural Perspective
1. form
2. symphony ; quartet
3. tempo ; molto ; meno
4. adagio ; vivo / vivace / presto
5. virtuosi (or virtuosos)
6. the Greeks / Classical Antiquity / the Greek idea of Drama
7. genre
8. waltz
9. concerto ; like a battle (combative) / dynamic / highly interactive
10. does not

Unit 4: Fanfare and Power: the Court of Louis XIV
1. church, court, theater
2. The Sun King ; anything that was elegant or modern in fashion or décor (such as hairstyles, shoes, mirrors, even folding umbrellas)

3.   false step (in court dancing) ; a symbol of dynastic power / proof of someone's intelligence and ability (etc.)
4.   The son of a king
5.   Hall of Mirrors ; to control completely his courtiers' lives / to impress everyone in Europe with his power
6.   1661 -1715 ; as the model of an absolute monarch
7.   Alexander the Great ; court painter
8.   harpsichord ; brilliant sound / beautifully decorated and elegant in appearance
9.   astronomy ; Galileo (or Copernicus, earlier but okay), Harvey (etc.)
10.   a great French playwright ; Lully

Unit 5: Sweeping Away the Renaissance Into the Baroque
1.   recitative ; aria
2.   a little book—text of an opera ; libro (Latin for book)
3.   monody ; polyphony
4.   c. 1600 – c. 1900
5.   two players ; chording instrument (keyboard, guitar, or lute) and sustaining low bass instrument (cello, bassoon)
6.   Renaissance
7.   fugue
8.   work ; Orfeo ; music conquers the power of death!
9.   lieto fine ; happy
10.   Monteverdi ; writing madrigals, motets, masses, music in polyphonic style

Unit 6: Liturgical Calendar, Street Parties, and the New Church Music
1.   liturgical
2.   Advent ; liturgical calendar
3.   the Bible / Saints' lives / the Apocrypha
4.   cantata
5.   Carnival ; Mardi gras ; in masks (masques) and costumes
6.   Fasnacht / Fat Tuesday / Shrove Tuesday
7.   passions
8.   before ; because the theaters were shut during Lent ; during ; the stories were appropriate for a penitential (fasting) season
9.   acting / costumes / sets / staging
10.   George Friedrich Handel ; Messiah

Unit 7: A Lively Journey Through the Life of Johann Sebastian Bach
1.   Vivaldi
2.   so many people in his family had a first name of Johann
3.   Doctrine of the Affections
4.   palace ; Frederick the Great
5.   C.P.E. Bach
6.   London
7.   the places where he worked / Leipzig
8.   boys' choir
9.   coffee houses
10.   Buxtehude ; walked / stayed much longer than he was supposed to

Unit 8: Enlightenment, Classicism, and the Astonishing Mozart
1. Leopold Mozart, Mozart's father
2. Diderot / Voltaire / Rousseau
3. Joseph Haydn
4. Rococo
5. Empfindsamkeit
6. clavichord
7. fortepiano / pianoforte
8. opera buffa ; commedia dell' arte
9. Da Ponte ; Don Giovanni ; jolly drama
10. The Creation

UNIT 9: Into the Abyss: The Century Struggles with Unfettered Imagination
1. Napoleon
2. Boethius ; musica mundana ; musica humana ; musica instrumentalis
3. Romantic
4. the novel ; novella ; epistolary novel
5. fairy tales (folk tales)
6. comfortable or pleasant
7. Sir Walter Scott ; Mary Shelley
8. Edgar Allan Poe
9. E.T. A. Hoffmann
10. Goethe ; Sorrows of Young Werther ; Faust ; the Devil and a professor (or, a bargain between the Devil and God, because the professor is caught in the middle)

Unit 10: Beethoven as Hero and Revolutionary
1. Caspar David Friedrich
2. Napoleon
3. Napoleon was crowned Emperor in 1804
4. a letter Beethoven wrote from the town of Heiligenstadt in 1802 where he was seeking treatment for his deafness.
5. his two brothers: it's not clear why because it seems partly like a last will and testament, a bit like a suicide note. It's filled with Romantic, poetic images.
6. a repeating pattern of pitches and rhythms used to characterize something
7. Fidelio ; rescue / redemption
8. monumentalism
9. the planet Uranus
10. musical sketches (his musical ideas recorded on paper)

Unit 11: Salons Poetry, and the Power of the Song
1. Lied (plural Lieder)
2. a salon (a formal front room, parlor, drawing room)
3. Biedermeier
4. Fanny Mendelssohn Hensel
5. Leipzig ; a cloth trading house, into which was put a space for concerts.
6. Felix Mendelssohn
7. Johann von Goethe
8. The poem must have a narrator and characters who "speak." It should begin and end abruptly, with no moral judgment at the end.
9. Erlkönig ; sick / ill /dying

10.   Schubert ; salons

Unit 12: A Tale of Four Virtuosi and the Birth of the Tone Poem
1.   Paganini
2.   Liszt
3.   Chopin
4.   night music, so it starts out peacefully and lyrically
5.   Polonaise or Mazurka
6.   étude
7.   Delacroix
8.   Jenny Lind ; toured U.S. with circus owner P.T. Barnum
9.   Berlioz ; an English Shakespearean actress (Harriet Smithson) whom he loved
10.   instrumental composition that describes a story, picture, or idea using musical sound (also, refer back to definition in unit)

Unit 13: Nationalism and the Explosion of Romantic Opera
1.   French Grand Opera
2.   en pointe
3.   bel = beautiful, canto = singing
4.   verismo
5.   minuet
6.   waltz
7.   sing + play = a staged play with singing ; musical
8.   Verdi
9.   O Holy Night
10.   Der Freischütz ; The main character goes to a dark part of the forest and watches as seven magic bullets are cast. He doesn't realize that one of these will strike his sweetheart.

Unit 14: The Absolutely New World of Wagner
1.   Ludwig II of Bavaria (a.k.a."Mad Ludwig" or "The Dream King")
2.   Wartburg Castle
3.   Gesamt = collected + Kunst = art + Werk = work
4.   a signature theme or guiding theme throughout a piece of music
5.   a singer in Medieval times who competed in singing competitions
6.   Festival Play House—Wagner's name for his opera house ; in Bayreuth, Bavaria (Southern Germany) ; so he could try out his revolutionary ideas for theater
7.   It had no boxes (where, in other theaters, the "special" and rich people would sit) / simple decoration (so that all attention would be on the stage) / no aisles (so people can't gather and chit-chat during performances) / a special orchestra pit extending beneath the stage for blending the orchestra's big sound.
8.   Adolph Hitler
9.   Switzerland ; he was in exile because of his political activity in Dresden.
10.   Rhine River

Unit 15: Imperial Russia – A Cultural Odyssey
1.   Tchaikovsky
2.   "Right or Correct" + "Bearer of, or Carrier of" – thus, the "bearer of the correct " or "carrier of the true and right."
3.   Italian ; Bortniansky ; Ukranian

4.   Mighty Fistful / Mighty Handful / Mighty Five ; professions outside of music such as sailor, scientist, civil clerk
5.   bells ; Bolshevik ; 1917
6.   an organization of mostly Russian artists who presented elaborate and exotic stage performances ; Paris
7.   Glinka
8.   an image that acts as a symbol, representing something bigger ; written ; read; venerated
9.   realistic pictures that showed hardships of life faced by the majority of Russians, especially serfs
10.   Moscow

Unit 16: Load Up the Wagons: The Story of American Music.
1.   singing of hymns ; singing of the Psalms (and the tunes used to do so)
2.   Appalachian regions, originally English, Irish, Welsh
3.   from Chinese laborers brought over to work on the railroads
4.   shape-note notation
5   New Orleans
6.   Charles Ives
7.   Stephen Foster
8.   the march
9.   Moravians
10.   Florenz Ziegfeld ; The Lion King

Unit 17: Turning the Page on Western Tradition with the Explosion of War
1.   end of the 19th Century. (It could be the end of any century but here refers to the end of the 19th century.)
2.   Schönberg / Schoenberg
3.   Debussy ; no
4.   Manet / Monet / Cezanne / Pissaro / Degas / Renoir
5.   Expressionism
6.   Vienna, capital of Austria
7.   fascination with things Chinese, or by extension, things Asian and/or exotic
8.   World War I
9.   Brahms
10.   In Flanders Field

SUGGESTED ANSWERS FOR VIEWING GUIDES

UNIT 1: USING MUSIC HISTORY TO UNLOCK WESTERN CULTURE

Please see the Listening Exercises (in lieu of a Viewing Guide).

UNIT 2: MUSIC ENTWINED WITH GREAT EVENTS IN WESTERN HISTORY

1. 1920s ; the songs played on the radio determined which songs would be popular ; now it's possible to hear virtually any kind of music.
2. Printing press in Mainz, Germany ; Gutenberg ; paper ; parchment.
3. Chinese
4. hand-copying done by trained people, often monks
5. animal skins ; 300
6. 30,000 ; nine million
7. by hand ; in manuscript (by copyists working in scriptoria).
8. no
9. mapmakers
10. backwards
11. lithography
12. At first it made songs even more popular, so people were still buying sheet music. But since it was now possible to hear music without learning to play and sing it, the gramophone hurt music publishing.
13. New York City ; music publishing
14. From the clanking piano sounds floating out of the windows of publishing houses, where songwriters presented new songs, hoping for publication.
15. acoustics
16. Pythagoras ; Aristotle
17. Greek theater builders considered acoustics / Medieval architects placed big ceramic urns to affect acoustics, etc.
18. French ; sun ; Classical mythology and Apollo.
19. Copernicus ; Kepler
20. Enlightenment ; the supernatural / the individual / the emotional / the psychological / the sublime

UNIT 3: TECHNOLOGY, TERMINOLOGY, AND CULTURAL PERSPECTIVE

1. shape, structure, construction, design (based on repetition and contrast)
2. buildings, architecture in general, any physical space or object
3. distinct sections within a larger piece of music
4. top left, above where the music itself begins
5. happy
6. walking tempo
7. at ease (slowly) ; broadly
8. fast ; vivere (to live)
9. meno ; molto
10. No. In earlier eras (Renaissance, Baroque), tempos or speeds were "understood" based on the kind of music being performed. It was an issue of style.
11. a champion athlete such as an Olympic gymnast or pole vaulter

12.   style

13.   kind or type of thing. (It comes from the Latin *genus,* meaning birth, family, or nation.)

14.   These things frequently overlap. A piece may be called one thing, but function as another thing. Plus the meanings of these genres may change throughout history, or from one composer to another. A composer can call a piece anything he or she wishes, in fact!

15.   large

16.   No, as long as there are four players (or even singers).

17.   Greeks (Greek drama)

18.   to agree / to harmonize / to reach an accord together

19.   It depends. It can be small (5 - 10 players), or medium sized (20 - 30 players), or as big as the modern orchestra (c. 100 players) or even bigger (orchestra and choirs combined). Generally speaking, ensembles have increased in size throughout Western music history, at least until the First World War, when almost everything drew back in size and scope. Today a modern orchestra will be about 85-100 players.

UNIT 4: FANFARE AND POWER: THE COURT OF LOUIS XIV

1.   Church, Court, and Theater

2.   We choose to hear voluntary music, either by playing it or turning on a piece of technology, from an MP3 player to a radio. Involuntary music comes to us whether we want it or not, in an elevator, while waiting in line, from the TV or from a car parked next to us.

3.   Women weren't allowed to sing in public

4.   Louis XIV

5.   Kapellmeister

6.   harpsichord

7.   Absolutism ; Louis XIV / Frederick the Great / Catherine the Great / Joseph II of Austria

8.   château ; hunting lodge

9.   dancers, singers, musicians, painters, costume and set designers, stage directors, etc.

10.   Sun King ; Classical Mythology and Apollo

11.   Charles Le Brun

12.   solar system ; establish an Academy of Science

13.   dancer ; faux pas ; the dance steps stayed simple enough for the King

14.   The Hall of Mirrors ; the signing of the treaties that ended both the Franco-Prussian War and the First World War

15.   Molière

16.   rising and dressing, and preparing for sleep at night

17.   French Overture

18.   Versailles ; palace interior ; gardens

UNIT 5: SWEEPING AWAY THE RENAISSANCE INTO THE BAROQUE

1.   Common Practice Era ; was "practiced" (played, performed, and perceived in a certain way)

2.   (choose three) Music had a clear pulse / musical scales were reduced to two scales—we call them major and minor / music had a clear melody line supported by a bass line / music was composed in specific, predictable forms, created by sections of contrast and repetition / music was played on the same instruments we more or less recognize today / these instruments were played in a traditional manner, appropriate to the instrument.

3.   Florence ; Dante / Boccaccio / Brunelleschi / da Vinci

4.   opera

5.   rebirth

6.   Humanism

7.   Monteverdi ; highly polyphonic (complex web of melody lines) ; monophonic (monody, or single melody line—recitative style)

8.   Fable (favola) in music.

9.   play ; sung

10.   choosing specific instruments to get the desired sound

11.   St. Mark's Cathedral

12.   A beloved mythological figure whose powers to charm through music and poetry were legendary. He was the son either of a Thracian king or the god Apollo, depending on the version. His mother was one of the Muses, Calliope.

13.   lieto fine

14.   Greek mythology / Classical history

15.   misshapen pearl ; was not

16.   single-line melody, or one musical line is sung ; manuscript ; polyphonic (with two, three, then four melody lines sounding simultaneously)

17.   two players, one playing a chording instrument, like a lute, harpsichord, organ and the other playing an instrument like a cello or bassoon, which can play a sustained bass line.

18.   toccata ; fantasia

19.   highly developed piece of music where a melody is presented and imitated in several voices

20.   information ; the part where the emotions are sung / set to melody

21.   opera seria ; intermezzos (intermezzi)

22.   the aristocracy, kings, noblemen: in short, only the rich

23.   opus ; opera

UNIT 6: LITURGICAL MUSIC, STREET PARTIES, AND THE NEW CHURCH MUSIC

1.   sacred ; secular ; it is associated with church performance or has a recognized part in the worship service.

2.   he wanted the new Protestant songs (hymns) to be lively, inspiring, and accessible, so he looked to popular and folk tunes.

3.   a worship service (church service); communion (also known as The Lord's Supper, Bread and Wine, or the Eucharist)

4.   the Feast days, or days of celebration within the church year ; Christmas or All Saints' Day; Easter, Good Friday, Maundy Thursday, Palm Sunday, Ash Wednesday

5.   it was hot, and there was a danger of spreading diseases ; Lent was a season of fasting and penitence (devotion).

6.   indulge in rich foods and lots of entertainment beforehand ; opera ; because opera is a social, glamorous, and extravagant art form ; masked balls

7.   New Orleans ; the region was settled by French Catholics, so the Liturgical Calendar shaped social life and entertainment.

8.   new operas ; new oratorios ; oratorios had no staging or acting, so they were appropriate for penitential (fasting) seasons.

9.   church itself (not in the services) ; within the church services (Protestant or Lutheran services)

10.   two ; a type of sermon

11.   Old Testament ; they are more dramatic. They have events like the bestowing of the Ten Commandments, the Parting of the Red Sea, plus many floods, battles, murders, assassinations, struggles of all kinds.
12.   Passions

UNIT 7: A LIVELY JOURNEY THROUGH THE LIFE OF JOHANN SEBASTIAN BACH.

1.   middle ; Sebastian ; first ; Johann
2.   Doctrine ; Affections ; stay joyful ; switch to something sad, dark, slow
3.   Stations ; outgrew his jobs, or was too advanced or modern for them, or was not permitted to write the kinds of music he wanted to compose
4.   Weimar ; church organist or church musician ; he sought a new job without permission to do so.
5.   Cöthen (Köthen) ; the music-loving duke died
6.   Leipzig ; boys in the boys' choir ; St. Thomas Church (Thomaskirche) ; Coffee Houses ; public concert
7.   organ ; bellows boys ; bellows ; air ; pipes ; electricity (electric motors)
8.   clavichord ; was not ; it was too soft to hear ; control the volume (dynamics) or sensitivity of each sound
9.   C.P.E. Bach ; Frederick the Great ; Berlin ; fortepiano (or pianoforte)

UNIT 8: ENLIGHTENMENT, CLASSICISM, AND THE ASTONISHING MOZART

1.   high skill level, increased complexity, and musical ideas all expanding, and then, suddenly, a collapse to a much simpler style.
2.   classical
3.   Alberti bass
4.   Monarchs (Monarchy) ; Prussia ; Russia ; Austria
5.   Art and artifacts from the Classical World – Ancient Greece and Rome, plus, for that matter, Ancient Egypt (by the way, this is not stated in the Unit Lecture, but it's fun to know☺)
6.   rococo
7.   galant ; pleasantness, naturalness, diversion, light-hearted emotion ; Watteau
8.   Sturm und Drang
9.   sensitive ; Affections
10.   sons ; Prussian ; Frederick the Great
11.   clavichord
12.   the hammer, the padding on the hammer, the tuning pins, the bridge, the sounding board, the escapement mechanism (double-escapement), the cast-iron frame
13.   harpsichord ; fortepiano (pianoforte) ; upright piano
14.   Thomas Jefferson
15.   Prague (today's Czech Republic)
16.   Italian (Italianate) ; France
17.   clarinet
18.   Turkish
19.   buffa ; seria; Singspiel ; The Magic Flute
20.   Lorenzo da Ponte ; The Marriage of Figaro (Le nozze di Figaro)
21.   He worked contentedly for many years for Count Esterhàzy. He enjoyed job stability and handled being a "servant" well.
22.   symphonies ; baryton

23.   Let there be Light (very quiet chorus leading up to it, and then a huge burst of sound on the word "light")

UNIT 9: INTO THE ABYSS: THE CENTURY STRUGGLES WITH UNFETTERED IMAGINATION

1.   literature
2.   the supernatural, the other-worldly, the spooky ; histories ; legends and folk or fairy tales ; works of art like operas, plays, paintings, novels, poems
3.   (choose) vernacular language of French, or any language related to French, and later any language stemming from Latin, a medieval verse or prose work, especially concerned with chivalry, a novel, an adventure story, or even "the sublime" or things that we cannot fully understand or explain, but know are real. Another answer would be art that doesn't have direct models in Classical Antiquity.
4.   Charles Dickens ; A Tale of Two Cities ; "It was the best of times; it was the worst of times."
5.   The Enlightenment ; coronated ; Notre Dame
6.   David ; Russia (Moscow) ; 1812 ; burning Moscow and leaving Napoleon and his troops without supplies for the winter ; Hitler (the Germans)
7.   Biedermeier ; Spitzweg ; Gemütlichkeit ; Congress of Vienna
8.   turned to extreme emotions / described the world around them, etc. ; emotional, supernatural, fantastic, even dangerous (threatening)
9.   musica mundana ; spheres; musica humana ; musica instrumentalis
10.   E.T.A. Hoffmann ; Mozart ; "inexpressible longing"; The Nutcracker
11.   Sir Walter Scott ; Lord George Gordon Byron ; Mozart
12.   The Grimm Brothers (The Brothers Grimm) ; they are about bewitched and fantastic creatures, supernatural, the battle of Good against Evil, villains, and spooks.
13.   Frankenstein ; The Raven ; Edgar Allan Poe
14.   madness (insanity) ; Lucia di Lammermoor
15.   Goethe ; The Sorrows (Sufferings) of Young Werther ; epistolary novel ; one way ; suicide ; Werther
16.   Weimar ; well ; Faust ; bargain (bet or wager) ; Devil (Mephistopheles, Mefisto) ; Devil; moment (day) of pure joy and contentment ; Devil ; soul
17.   Schiller

UNIT 10: BEETHOVEN AS HERO AND REVOLUTIONARY

1.   he represents a new kind of "Romantic" artist—an individual struggling against society, a genius whose talents were too great to be fully appreciated. He was a hero whose music (posthumously) became a new standard against which other music would be compared.
2.   18—specifically 5 months shy of 19 (he was born 16 December 1770`; the French Revolution begins July 14, 1789)
3.   the patronage system where a count, for example, would determine his career
4.   Not exceptionally
5.   He was not well connected, he didn't have the proper upbringing or preparation socially for the big city, his temperament rebelled against the role that was expected of him.
6.   Johann von Goethe ; no, they did not agree on many things, including the appropriate way to defer to aristocracy.
7.   At first he was thrilled, but he was later disappointed when Napoleon began grabbing power and crowned himself Emperor.

8.   A rescue opera (or Singspiel) ; four overtures

9.   the loyalty of a wife, bravery in face of danger, political oppression, hope triumphing over desperation, the excitement of a last-minute rescue

10.   more difficult for audiences, more extreme, more introverted, less automatically attractive, less likely to please

11.   sitting on a "throne" like a god of some kind, with an eagle, and all kinds of monumental symbols

12.   It was done years later, and it shows the powerful figure Beethoven had become— no longer a man who wrote music, but a kind of god-like figure who towered over the world of music, knowing all, seeing all, directing all!

13.   Healing City ; to seek a cure for his deafness ; Testament ; it is both a difficult-to-understand letter, possibly a suicide letter that tells us much about Beethoven's state of mind, and a statement of the new "Romantic" views of nature, God, and fate.

14.   manicured, sculpted, trimmed Baroque gardens ; open, free, wild, overgrown "Romantic" parks (although still trimmed by gardeners to get the right look!).

15.   longer, bigger, more monumental in scope, more intense harmonies, dark, sometimes heroic, and always emotional, very specific indications, unexpected structure and unexpected passages, less lyrical and more dependent on patterns (motives) that aren't really melodies, making his own rules.

16.   In his later works, he also put these terms into the vernacular (his own language of German) rather than just Italian.

17.   sketches ; his musical and compositional ideas (drawn out in notes), his creative processes

18.   The moon was mysterious, sublime, inexplicable, plus the moon made a mesmerizing focal point. And people were very interested in the moon, astronomically, in those days.

19.   Father of Modern Astronomy ; Uranus

UNIT 11: SALONS, POETRY, AND THE POWER OF THE SONG

1.   lute ; Queen Elizabeth of England ; 1603 ; Shakespeare ; John Dowland

2.   "words carefully chosen and arranged on a page."

3.   The audience must understand the words; the words should connect emotionally with the listener; the song needs to be presented in an appropriate environment.

4.   small or intimate

5.   read aloud as a poem ; set to music as a song

6.   the supernatural, lost love or disappointed love, nature, legends, adventure stories, Medieval themes, folk themes

7.   a parlor or room where invited guests would gather to hear the newest poetry and literature read, and to enjoy the newest pieces of music

8.   It has a narrator; it has actual characters who address one another; it narrates objectively and begins in media res—suddenly, without a lot of explanation.

9.   in the middle of things or midstream

10.   four ; the father, the boy, the Erl-King, and the narrator (and if you count the horse, you get a fifth character☺)

11.   early 19th century

12.   He was frustrated in his attempts to marry Clara Wieck, so the bitter story would have appealed to him (plus Heine was a great poet).

13.   The happiness doesn't last, and the poems become progressively sadder or angrier.

14.   "I don't complain" ; using low, pounding chords, setting up an insistent and angry musical accompaniment

15.   the poet's resignation to the situation, and a beautiful piano postlude.

UNIT 12: A TALE OF FOUR VIRTUOSI AND THE BIRTH OF THE TONE POEM

1.   the excitement of watching someone do something physically "impossible" and the glamour and star status of such people (for example, super-star athletes)

2.   Paganini

3.   He had an usual appearance, especially his hands, and people were fascinated by him. He seemed to be self taught, which gave rise to the rumor that "the devil" had taught him. Also, his technique in playing the violin was radical and new, plus performances by solo virtuosi were, themselves, very new. The Romantic era promoted the idea of the "creative individual" and virtuosi fit the bill!

4.   A human achievement, something from "beyond" or even the supernatural. A gift a person was born with, largely unexplained. Art had a secret message for us, and only artists could understand certain things. Artists were no longer servants and craftsmen, but specially endowed visionaries who could point the way into the future.

5.   fifteen

6.   Franz Liszt

7.   was elegant, handsome, charming to the ladies.

8.   concert pianist, recitalist, performer ; Europe and even Russia

9.   Chopin, George Sands, Delacroix

10.   City of Lights ; He had started the idea of public street lighting with candles and torches. This public lighting gave Paris its first nightlife and made it the envy of Europe.

11.   Weimar ; compose more, especially tone poems ; Rome ; focus on religious study and preparation, ultimately becoming an Abbé

12.   brilliant virtuoso performers ; Jenny Lind ; Sweden

13.   It was more poetic, more subdued, less bombastic, less concentrated on thrills and more on expression (although there were plenty of thrills). Also Chopin didn't have a career as a public, touring virtuoso, the way they did.

14.   to study ; a piece used as an exercise in order to master difficult performing techniques

15.   Polish ; Paris

16.   no

17.   a piece of instrumental music that tries to paint a picture of something, either a place, a thing, an atmosphere, or even an emotion

18.   Irish ; John Field

19.   works like symphonies, operas, string quartets, oratorios

20   Jewish

21.   St. Paul ; Elijah

22.   J.S. Bach

23.   painter, or watercolorist

24.   Fanny Mendelssohn Hensel

25.   the orchestra conductor

26.   music performed by a variety of players, including singers, violinists and pianists, small ensembles, wind and brass players too! It was more like a variety show.

27.   instrumental pieces that tell a story (without words) or describe (paint in music) a place, person, thing, or emotion

28.   Hector Berlioz ; his passion for an English Shakespearean actress named Harriet Smithson

29.   A house where Liszt lived, above Weimar, and a lot of his friends and fellow musicians visited and also stayed. It was a "creative" center, you might say.

30.   His ideas were more advanced than the people around him. He did not write operas, but he conducted operas. He also conducted controversial music, both his and the new music of other composers.

31.   Richard Wagner

UNIT 13: NATIONALISM AND THE EXPLOSION OF ROMANTIC OPERA

1.   Louis XIV ; minuet ; waltz

2.   to dance

3.   Beethoven

4.   Romantic ; Classical ; Classical ; Romantic

5.   the spooky, supernatural, Gothic, mysterious

6.   Sentimentalism ; Gothic, supernatural ; Willis

7.   mad ; Lucia di Lammermoor ; Sir Walter Scott

8.   motives

9.   French ; [French] Grand ; weddings, processionals, coronations, feasts

10.   the supernatural, the spooky, the mysterious ; rescue or redemption

11.   1821 ; it featured lots of German folk elements, like the forest, hunting, folk dancing, and the sound of a men's chorus (*Männerchor*). It also used several well-known German superstitions, which caught the attention of the audience.

12.   Franco-Prussian War ; 1870-71 ; 1861

13.   musical (Broadway musical)

14.   "Ordinary" opera has sung recitatives (that is, information or conversation will be sung in rhythmically free melody). In Singspiel, or dialogue opera, the information, or conversation is spoken, as in a play. In both forms, the arias (songs), duets, and choruses are sung.

15.   Absolutely not! (There are many tragic and sad endings.)

16.   Rossini, Donizetti, Bellini

17.   *bel* = beautiful + *canto* = singing, so "beautiful singing"

18.   overtures ; ensembles

19.   King Nebuchadnezzar ; "Va pensiero" (Fly, Thoughts, on Wings of Gold)

20.   A longer scene in an opera (started in 19th century) which weaves arias, duets, choruses together, more or less seamlessly

21.   The fight by Italian nationalists to overthrow Austrian power and unify Italy into a country.

22.   Viva Vittorio Emanuele, King (Re) of (d') Italy (Italia) ; To make a cry in public for an Italian King (and a united national Italy) was politically dangerous. Using Verdi's name as a "code" was safer.

23.   Spanish.

24.   with the on-stage murder of Carmen ; verismo

25.   The Metropolitan Opera Saturday Matinees (from New York City); Texaco

UNIT 14: THE ABSOLUTELY NEW WORLD OF WAGNER

1.   Rhine river (or the gold from the Rhine, or the problems of the gods from Valhalla) ; Germanic, Nordic (or Scandanavian)

2.   less than ideal, somewhat unstable, artistic through his stepfather

3.   false
4.   Hitler was enthusiastic about Wagner's music and the ideas in his essays.
5.   The Flying Dutchman ; he was caught in a storm while fleeing his position at Riga because of his debts.
6.   not successful or pleasant: he couldn't break in
7.   Wartburg ; 1517 ; translate the New Testament ; competed in the famous Medieval "Singers' Wars."
8.   Gesamtkunstwerk
9.   Franz Liszt ; Bavarian King Ludwig II (Mad Ludwig, or The Dream King)
10.   Leitmotiv (leading or guiding motive) ; characters, things, and ideas
11.   underneath ; the huge sound of his big orchestra would not overwhelm the singers on stage, but would blend together and make a perfect balance with their voices ; Wagner tuba
12.   false (He wanted their ears, brains, and imaginations fully engaged!)
13.   19 ; was not
14.   Das Rheingold ; his operas needed to be seen, heard, and experienced completely, and short excerpts on a CD cannot give us that experience (so excerpts would probably be upsetting to him☺).
15.   false
16.   true

UNIT 15: IMPERIAL RUSSIA—A CULTURAL ODYSSEY

1.   Orthodoxy, or Eastern Christianity
2.   ortho ; right, correct, true; dox/ doxos ; carrier of/bearer of
3.   a capella ; fluid
4.   Old Believers
5.   bells
6.   icons ; worshipped ; to look upon with respect and reverence
7.   seven ; Italian ; Empresses (Tsarinas) Anna, Elizabeth, and Catherine the Great
8.   Ukrainian ; birthplace (original site)
9.   Father of Russian Music ; it used an important Russian historical story, the sound of Russian a capella church singing, folk rhythms and melodies, and it came along just at the right time.
10.   serfdom ; 1861
11.   Chekhov; Seagull, Cherry Orchard, Three Sisters ; Stanislavsky ; acting
12.   The Wanderers, Itinerants, Peredvizhniki ; serfs ; aristocracy or royalty ; Repin
13.   Pushkin ; verse ; Eugene Onegin ; Tatiana ; in a duel
14.   Tchaikovsky ; Mighty Handful (Mighty Five, Mighty Fistful, Moguchaia kuchka) ; Tchaikovsky ; tone poems, Russian operas on historical themes, and anything that would give the flavor of Old Russia
15.   Pictures at an Exhibition ; Promenade ; Baba Yaga ; chicken legs
16.   Boris Godunov ; Rurik ; Romanov ; guilty conscience, or fear of the murdered Rurik prince returning ; coronation
17.   Russian speech (Russian language) ; mad
18.   sailor ; orchestrator ; St. Petersburg Conservatory ; didn't know enough ; Flight of the Bumblebee
19.   son ; Stravinsky
20.   Rachmaninov ; America ; a beloved pianist who toured across America many times.

21.   Scriabin ; color in music , or electricity ; a color wheel to be triggered at different places in his compositions ; Bolshevik Revolution ; Lenin
22.   Ballets russes ; Russian dance or exotic ballets ; Parisians (the French)
23.   Stravinsky ; Firebird ; puppet ; Petrushka ; Nijinsky
24.   Revolutions ; February ; October ; October Revolution or Bolshevik Revolution ; Lenin ; destroying Russian Christianity and destroying many of the roots of Russian culture, including folk culture

UNIT 16: LOAD UP THE WAGONS: THE STORY OF AMERICAN MUSIC

1.   a complete tradition of Native American music already here ; oral ; genres
2.   Regionalism
3.   Fiddle tunes ; Appalachian
4.   1622 ; Christianity ; reading, writing, singing ; Latin
5.   Psalmody ; Psalms
6.   Moravians ; North Carolina ; organ
7.   Shape-note ; America was "taught to sing" by traveling singing masters who set up singing schools.
8.   Joy to the World; (choose) My Faith Looks Up to Thee, When I Survey the Wondrous Cross, Blest Be the Tie That Binds, O For a Thousand Tongues to Sing
9.   March ; opera or operetta
10.   ladies ; husbands ; courts, kings, royalty, aristocracy
11.   circus
12.   Europe
13.   George ; band master and choir director ; know that he composed
14.   hymn tunes, melodies from operas and symphonies, march tunes, folk songs, popular songs, etc. ; 114 Songs
15.   Canadian Army Doctor (and Lieutenant Colonel); red poppy ; war dead
16.   Mardi gras ; that part of America was settled by French Catholics who observed the Liturgical Calendar, and, therefore, held many parties before Lent began ; First City
17.   Chinese ; railroads
18.   1843 ; Northern ; black-face ; songs, jokes, tap dancing, tricks, animal acts, and the preferred variety-show format in American entertainment
19.   Stephen Foster ; O Susanna, Beautiful Dreamer, Camptown Races, I Dream of Jeannie with the Light Brown Hair, etc.; banjo
20.   decreased ; Vaudeville
21.   Irving Berlin ; Russia ; was not ; Alexander's Ragtime Band
22.   Ziegfeld ; New Amsterdam ; Walt Disney Corp. ; The Lion King

UNIT 17: TURNING THE PAGE ON WESTERN TRADITION AND THE EXPLOSION OF WAR.

1.   fin-de-siécle ; 19th
2.   A Nervous Splendor
3.   Johannes Brahms, Gustav Mahler, Richard Strauss, Arnold Schönberg, Sigmund Freud, Gustav Klimt, and, of course, Emperor Franz Joseph
4.   Ringstrasse ; the huge buildings show wealth, stability, power at a time when much of the social order was crumbling and current events were leading toward World War I.
5.   The Scream ; Edvard Munch

6.   he continued with the traditional "classical" structures inherited from Haydn, Mozart, and Beethoven, writing symphonies, concertos, sonatas, and staying within the musical vocabulary of the Common Practice Era.

7.   Beethoven

8.   idiomatic

9.   Clara Wieck Schumann

10.   Jewish ; convert to Christianity ; Alma (Schindler) ; quit composing ; the death of a little daughter

11.   he added many more players to the orchestra. He added vocal soloists and choirs to his symphonies, plus increased the size of the choirs. He used new sounds, including odd percussion (like anvils). He contrasted huge sounds with delicate sounds. He made listeners hear orchestral music in a new way.

12.   the dominance of German music

13.   Impressionist ; he was a contemporary of the Impressionist painters, who chose not to write in traditional forms, but to paint pictures in musical sound, using soft lines, getting rid of a strong pulse, and using a beautiful palate of orchestral sounds ; Symbolist ; words

14.   Impression: Sunrise ; Monet ; was not

15.   Wagner or Wagnerism

16.   chinoiserie ; Turandot ; Madame Butterfly ; stabs (murders) ; jumps to her death (commits suicide)

17.   world's fairs

18.   Richard Strauss ; tone poems ; opera conductor ; operas ; Salome

19.   to build little tubes (connected to water bottles) into the "rocks" at the back of the set!

20.   electricity

21.   hiking into remote villages to hear the folksongs ; gramophone

22.   Romantic ; Verklärte Nacht (Transfigured Night) ; atonal ; radical, shocking, drastic ; did not

23.   singing

24.   Rite of Spring ; choreography ; Nijinsky ; distorted, jagged, against, or the opposite of, Classical ballet technique

25.   give it repeated hearings, so that your ear grows and develops, and comes to understand it.

AUDIO CDs

CD ONE

1 Dowland: Flow My Tears Steven Rickards, counter-tenor; Dorothy Linell, lute **4:03**

2 Monteverdi: *Orfeo*, Toccata San Petronio Cappella Musicale Orchestra, Sergio Vartolo, cond. **1:44**

3 Gabrieli, G.: Canzon septimi toni a 8 (No. 2) London Symphony Brass, Eric Crees, cond. **3:02**

4 Mouret: Rondeau John Roderick MacDonald, Trumpet; Martin Stephan, organ **1:52**

5 Lully: *Ballet d'Alcidiane et Polexandere*, Ouverture Arcadia Ensemble, Kevin Mallon, cond. **1:38**

6 Lully: *Ballet de Xerxes*, Bourrée pour les Basques Arcadia Ensemble **1:05**

7 Charpentier: Messe de Minuit pour Nöel, H.9 Sanctus and Benedictus Arcadia Ensemble **3:11**

8 Bach, J.S.: Toccata and Fugue in D minor, BWV 565 Wolfgang Rubsam, organ **9:22**

9 Bach: J.S.: Brandenburg Concerto No. 2 in F major, BWV 1047 I Allegro Swiss Baroque Soloists **4:49**

10 Bach, J.S.: Brandenburg Concerto No. 2 in F major, BWV 1047 II Andante Swiss Baroque Soloists **3:26**

11 Bach, J.S.: Brandenburg Concerto No. 2 in F major, BWV 1047 III Allegro assai Swiss Baroque Soloists **2:40**

12 Bach, J.S.: French Suite No. 5 in G major, BWV 816 Gavotte Laurence Cummings, harpsichord **1:02**

13 Bach, J.S.: Cantata 147 Chorus: Jesu, bleibet meine Freude Hungarian Radio Chorus. Budapest Failoni Chamber Orchestra, Matya Antal, cond. **3:23**

14 Bach, J.S.: *Coffee Cantata*, BWV 211 Recitative: Du böses Kind Budapest Failoni Chamber Orchestra, Matyas Antal, cond. **0:32**

15 Bach, J.S. *Coffee Cantata*, BWV 211 Aria: Ei! Wie schmeckt der Kaffee süsse Budapest Failoni Chamber Orchestra **3:55**

16 Handel: *Messiah* And He Shall Purify the Sons of Levi New College Choir, Oxford; Academy of Ancient Music, Edward Higginbottom, cond. **2:32**

17 Handel: Concerto Grosso No. 6 in D major, HWV 317 (op. 3) I Vivace Northern Sinfonia **2:42**

18 Bach, C.P.E.: *L'Philippine*, Wq. 117/34, H.96 Miklos Spanyi, clavichord **2:55**

19 Haydn: Trumpet Concerto in E-flat major, HOB VIIe: I Allegro Eklund Niklas, trumpet; Swedish Chamber Orchestra, Roy Goodman, cond. **6:44**

20 Mozart: Symphony No. 40 in G minor, K.550 I Allegro molto Capella Istropolitana, Barry Wordsworth, cond. **7:31**

21 Mozart: Piano Sonata No. 11 in A major, K.331 III Rondo alla turca Jeno Jando, piano **3:46**

CD TWO

1 Mozart: *Don Giovanni* Overture, K. 527 Capella Istropolitana, Barry Wordsworth, cond. **6:12**

2 Mozart: *Don Giovanni* Recitative: Alfin siam liberati Nicolaus Esterhazy Sinfonia, Michael Halasz, cond. **1:59**

3 Mozart: *Don Giovanni* Duet: La ci darem la mano Nicolaus Esterhazy Sinfonia, Michael Halasz, cond. **3:09**

4 Beethoven: Symphony No. 5, Op. 6 I Allegro con brio Zagreb Philharmonic, Richard Edlinger, cond. **6:56**

5 Beethoven: Piano Concerto No. 1, Op. 15 III Rondo Stefan Vladar, piano; Capella Istropolitana, Barry Wordsworth, cond. **8:47**

6 Schubert: Erlkönig Johannes Kalpers, tenor; Burkhard Kehring. piano **4:02**

7 Loewe: Erlkönig Hermann Prey, baritone; Michael Endres, piano **3:13**

8 Schumann: *Dichterliebe* Im wunderschönen Monat Mai Sebastian Bluth, baritone; Anita Keller, piano **1:23**

9 Schumann: *Dichterliebe* Im Rhein, im heiligen Strome Sebastian Bluth, baritone; Anita Keller, piano **2:22**

10 Schumann: *Dichterliebe* Ich grolle nicht Sebastian Bluth, baritone; Anita Keller, piano **1:41**

11 Schumann: *Dichterliebe* Die alten, bösen Lieder Sebastian Bluth, baritone; Anita Keller, piano **5:03**

12 Bizet: *Carmen* Habañera Graciela Alperyn, mezzo-soprano; Slovak Radio Symphony Orchestra, Alexander Rahbari, cond. **4:54**

13 Chopin: Etude Op. 12 No. 10 in C minor "Revolutionary" Peter Nagy, piano **2:57**

14 Chopin: Berceuse in D-flat major, Op. 57 Peter Nagy, piano **4:33**

15 Mendelssohn: *Songs without Words* Spinnerlied Book 6, Op. 67, No. 4 Peter Nagy, piano **1:51**

16 Paganini: Caprice in E major, Op. 1, No. 1 Ilya Kaler, violin **1:54**

17 Liszt: Transcendental Etude No. 10 in F minor "Appassionata" Jeno Jando, piano **4:52**

18 Wagner: *Das Rheingold* Vorspiel (Prelude) Stuttgart State Opera Orchestra, Lothar Zagrosek, cond. **4:25**

CD THREE

1 Brahms: Rhapsody in G minor, Op. 79, No. 2 Jeno Jando, piano **6:40**

2 Brahms: Wiegenlied, Op. 49, No. 4 Mitsuko Shirai, mezzo-soprano; Hartmut Holl, piano **2:16**

3 Kedrov: Otche nash (Our Father) Bulgarian National Choir, Georgi Robev, cond. **3:47**

4 Mussorgsky: *Pictures at an Exhibition* Promenade Jeno Jando, piano **1:26**

5 Mussorgsky: *Pictures at an Exhibition* Ballet of the Chicks Jeno Jando, piano **1:15**

6 Tchaikovsky: *1812 Overture*, Op. 49 Royal Philharmonic Symphony Orchestra, Adrian Leaper, cond. **15:32**

7 Grieg: *Peer Gynt* I Suite No. 1, Op. 46 Morning Mood BBC Scottish Symphony, Jerzy Maksymiuk, cond. **3:55**

8 Grieg: *Peer Gynt* IV Suite No. 1, Op. 46 In the Hall of the Mountain King BBC Scottish Symphony, Jerzy Maksymiuk, cond. **2:41**

9 Strauss: *Don Quixote* Thema - Knight of the Sorrowful Countenance Ireland National Symphony, Gerhard Markson, cond. **2:14**

10 Strauss: *Don Quixote* Variation II - Kriegerisch (The Battle of the Sheep) Ireland National Symphony **1:40**

11 Debussy: *Suite bergamasque* Clair de lune François-Joel Thiollier, piano **5:10**

12 Puccini: *Turandot* Nessun dorma Janez Lotric, tenor; Kiev Chamber Choir, Ukranian National Opera Symphony Orchestra, Johannes Wildner, cond. **3:10**

13 Mahler: Ich bin der Welt abhanden gekommen Hidenori Komatsu, baritone; Hanover Radio Philharmonic Orchestra, Cord Garben, cond. **6:59**

14 Vaughan Williams: The Call Simon Keenlyside, baritone; Graham Johnson, piano **2:17**

15 Stravinsky: *Firebird* Danse infernale Belgian Radio and Television Orchestra, Alexander Rahbari, cond. **4:40**

16 Sousa: Liberty Bell March Royal Swedish Airforce Band, Jerker Johansson, cond. **3:34**

17 Joplin: Maple Leaf Rag Alexander Peskanov, piano **3:11**

18 Ives: In Flanders Field Patrick Carfizzi, bass-baritone, J.J. Penna, piano **2:24**